Dr. Gerald Doggett



# Surviving the Challenges of Transition

## Nuggets to Remember on the Way to Your Dream

Parsons Publishing House
*Your Voice Your World*™
Stafford, VA USA

Surviving the Challenges of Transition
By Gerald Doggett

Parsons Publishing House
P. O. Box 488
Stafford, VA 22554 USA
www.ParsonsPublishingHouse.com
Info@ParsonsPublishingHouse.com



All Scripture quotations, unless otherwise indicated, are taken from the taken from the Holy Bible, King James Version, Cambridge, 1769.



International Standard Book Number:
13 digit: 978-1-60273-018-2
10 digit: 1-60273-018-0
Library of Congress Control Number: 2011941301
Printed in the United States of America.
Published by Parsons Publishing House
for World-Wide Distribution.

# TABLE OF CONTENTS

# ACKNOWLEDGEMENTS

To Darrell and Diane Parsons, dear friends for many years, who pushed me to finish this project. Your belief in my assignment remains a source of strength to my personal journey. Thanks to Diane for encouraging me through personal seasons of transition. Thanks to Darrell for providing a word in season that released much of the voyage we presently enjoy. Thanks to Brianna who remains a beautiful testimony of your Biblical guidance and for loaning me your Mom and Dad for this season. Darrell and Diane, your friendship is ever faithful, and I am grateful.

My beautiful wife, Doris, who always believes in me, and her prayers for our family have kept us alive for these many years. You are my Proverbs 31 Lady. Your strength and core values remain a rock of stability in my life. I am a better man because of you. Your prayerful intercession in private has made a difference in our ministry, as well as countless other areas of life. Our years together have taken us through many successful transitions. You will always be special to me. I love you.

# FOREWORD

Perhaps more than at any other time in history, the culture we live in is marked by uncertainty and unpredictability. The rapid pace of change due to everything from advances in technology to continental economic shifts and an unprecedented time of global shaking are the cause of it all. Navigating your way through the landscape of contemporary life now more than ever requires the ability to master the cycles and processes of transition.

While everything that can be shaken is indeed shaken in transition, the good news is that if you are a child of God, you have received a Kingdom that cannot be shaken. Given that truth, transition-mastery becomes the earmark of those who are led by the Spirit, the mature sons and daughters of God. The only way to attain transition-mastery, which includes among other things, letting go of a former chapter of your life that ended either expectedly or unexpectedly, moving through a territory without maps into a new chapter of your life and calling requires naked faith, and the courage to risk moving forward.

In transition, the nowhere in-between a former somewhere and a yet-to-be-revealed somewhere is the gap God is always seeking someone to stand in and fill who can build a bridge between where things once were to where things need to be. That gap between where you were and where you are headed is filled with potential and possibility when you discover your capacity to manage the transition by taking on a whole new dimension of thinking, feeling, speaking, and acting.

Old paradigms are destined to die in transition so that new paradigms can take their place. The radical disorientation of transition is designed to posture you for a new orientation that brings you into the experience of God's exceedingly abundant and beyond all that you can ask or think atmosphere of what wants to emerge in your life. It is in that precarious place of being in-between where you once were and where you are yet to be that you need to fix your "rememberer." There, in transition, the unchanging truth of the UNCHANGING PERSON of Christ needs to constantly be brought to your remembrance, because the God Who has been faithful before, will be faithful again, even in the seasons of transition.

Bishop Gerald Doggett is one of the most articulate and powerful communicators I know of in the Kingdom of God. His ability to take portions of Scripture and mine the gold that is in them, with apostolic wisdom and prophetic insight, provide the necessary ingredients to feed the flock of God with powerful, practical, and presently-effective learning strategies for success in your journey and calling in Christ.

This treatise you hold in your hands, ***Surviving the Challenges of Transition***, is a road atlas, a spiritual map, to help you chart the course and navigate your way through transition, master the emotions of change, and move into the new thing God is doing in your life. Take your time in each chapter and digest each morsel that Bishop Doggett serves you. You will discover that as you feed on each serving, you will assimilate strength, resolve, confidence, and faith for the journey and clarity will come, and your light will break forth like the noon-day sun. This is a life-long learning manual, take it with you wherever your path leads you, and you will find the Spirit of God using it to speak to you again, and again, and again.

Mark J. Chironna, M.A., Ph.D.
Pastor, The Master's Touch International Church
Orlando, Florida

# INTRODUCTION

Your dream is within your reach! You might think it's far away, but it's not as far as you might think. Just one more relationship connection, one more phone call, one more trip to the mail box, or one more idea could catapult your dream into the arena of manifestation!

Problem is you have your eyes on the difficult times you experience rather than the beautiful, full color, photo that God gave you at the beginning of this journey. Even if the difficult moments have surprised you; you can't stop at the difficulties because it wasn't in the dream. If the dream is yet to be experienced, you can't quit now; you must keep dreaming and keep walking toward fulfillment. You are just in a time we call TRANSITION!

*Transition* by definition means, "a passing from one condition, form, stage, activity, or place, to another; the period of such passing." Based on the definition of the word, there could be some difficulties encountered in the process. I'm sure that you have already walked through some of those difficult times in the experience we call LIFE!

I am keenly aware that during the process of discovering your God-given assignment, and the journey to the fulfillment of that assignment, you will find that life provides different conditions, forms, activities, places, and stages. It's how we navigate this journey that determines the final outcome of the dream God gave us at the beginning.

Some drop out of the process and feel sadness as they walk away from the dream God placed in their heart. There is always a feeling of sadness when you walk away from the will and plan God has for your life. It's a sadness that begins in your heart and moves into your mind and ultimately will affect your demeanor. You walk slower, head bent down, and lose energy as you wander through day after day with no direction or excitement.

Difficulties in understanding the seasons of transition can cause doubt and fear to take control and dominate the decision making process. When we make decisions out of a fear-filled heart there is anxiety and apprehension. On the other hand, making decisions out of a faith-filled heart reveals hope and the expectation of a desired outcome.

Life seems like one eternal transition. Problems surface when we face situations that are unfamiliar. Since we have not passed this way before, we often draw back and decide that because it's not familiar, it must not be the will of God. Discomfort is not always a sign you are out of the will of God, or that you are walking away from the dream God placed in your heart. In fact, if you are uncomfortable right now, it could be a signal that you are on the threshold of your greatest breakthrough!

When you evaluate great men and women of the Bible, they always seemed to be most uncomfortable immediately before God used them for His greatest purpose. In fact, these great people that have been the subject of many inspiring sermons and books lived lives outside their comfort zone for most of their journey. I know the Bible doesn't say they were uncomfortable; however, if you evaluate their mindset, you will conclude they were uncomfortable. It's not correct thinking to conclude we must distance ourselves from discomfort lest we offend God or make Him mad by being out of His will and plan for our life. Don't be afraid of a little discomfort, it could be the resistance that propels you to the next level of your dream.

As we move through the process of transitions, be sensitive to the ebb and flow of seasons and learn to maximize the moments of the journey so that we may experience the highest levels of joy and fulfillment. You might have to shift your mindset, change your thinking, and release your faith at another level, but it will be worth every effort.

Life is exciting; don't miss a moment by living in an emotional cave. Come on out and enjoy the journey. *TRANSITION* is a word that continues to introduce you to seasonal changes that release personal growth and reveal life's most exciting challenges. My prayer is that *SURVIVING THE CHALLENGES OF TRANSITION* will map strategies for personal triumphs and provide encouragement to the reader as this journey of life unfolds from day to day.

# CHAPTER 1

## DURING TRANSITION REMEMBER...

## IT'S OKAY TO REMAIN A CHAIR!

Time builds equity. If you were to go to the store a buy a valuable chair for a thousand dollars and keep that chair for a long time it would slowly decrease in value. When its value has declined to only a few dollars you could sell that chair in a yard sale for maybe fifty dollars to someone who knew the original value. Once purchased at the yard sale, the new owner keeps the chair, and as the years pass the value of the chair increases again until it surpasses the original value and becomes an antique or priceless collector's item.

What caused the chair to increase in value? It was time; time builds equity or value. All the chair had to do to increase in value was simply, "keep being a chair." That chair didn't wake up one day and say, "Chairs aren't worth much today so make me into a table." It just kept being a chair. Consistency to its original design brought an increase in value. I'm sure that some days it wasn't fun being a chair. Some days were painful, some days the chair was ignored, some days the chair was not treated fairly, and some days it might have been abused and used for other things.

Your life can be a lot like that chair. There are days you go through pain, some days you are ignored, some days you are not treated fairly, and some days you might even feel abused. Your challenge is to keep being the person God called you to be, and never abort the process that will ultimately bring your dream to fulfillment.

Be reminded again of the definition of *transition* which means, "a passing from one condition, form, stage, activity, place, to another, or the period of such passing." God has you in a process. *Process* means, "A continuing development involving many changes." It's the "many changes" that cause concern.

Always remember that change is constant, but it always has a direction, and that direction is your pull to the future. We have been conditioned to believe that all change is bad. All change is not bad. The process of change serves to develop you, as well as the dream in your heart.

It's okay to remain true to yourself and true to your assignment. Even during times of uncertainty stay focused on what God has spoken. External voices will entice you to do a complete makeover when it's simply not necessary.

Develop core values which provide a "character anchor" during periods of temptation and enticement. Be able to identify a value system connected to your recreated spirit that will provide power and tenacity during seasons of shifting values. Refuse to change in order to accommodate a temporary discomfort. **Be true to the value system found in God's Word.**

# CHAPTER 2

DURING TRANSITION REMEMBER...

## YOUR DREAM IS MORE THAN A PREDICTION OF YOUR FUTURE!

It is essential to remember that the personal "word of the Lord" that God speaks to your heart is not a predictive word. When God gives you a word it is not predicting what might happen if everything goes right. The psychic hotline can, at the very least, do that well.

Our belief system has eroded to where we have taken the prophetic word of God as a prediction of our future. Similar to the weather man who stands before a camera and gives a prediction about future weather based on certain information obtained by data and interpreted by experts. Most of the time it doesn't happen exactly like the weatherman says. The prophetic word of God can no longer be treated as a spiritual weather forecast. The word of the Lord is your guiding light during transition. It will illuminate your path, reveal pitfalls, and keep you on the road that must be traveled to achieve the completion of the dream.

When God speaks a personal word to you it is a creative word. When God talks, He creates! In Genesis, chapter one, God said, "Let there be light." God was not predicting light, He was creating light. An angel delivered a message, from God, to Mary concerning the conception and birth of a son. Mary said, "Be it unto me according to thy word" (Luke 1:38). The word spoken to her was creative. It was a word so powerful that it produced flesh and bone that was manifested as Jesus, the Son of God.

When you carry a word from God in your spirit, it is not predicting your future; it is ahead of you, creating your future. God is omnipresent. He is not only in today; He is also in yesterday and tomorrow. God is already in your tomorrow creating your desired future. Isaiah provides clear insight as to God's thoughts about your future. It's as though God provided the prophet with insights that can be used as a source of strength during transition.

> *Remember the former things of old: for I am God, and there is none else; I am God, and there is none like me, Declaring the end from the beginning, and from ancient times the things that are not yet*

*done, saying, My counsel shall stand, and I will do all my pleasure:* (Isaiah 46:9-10).

When this passage of Scripture says, "Declaring the end from the beginning," it is providing a mental photo of God standing right where you are today articulating just how the end will manifest. He knows, and is sure about the future; He will declare and make clearly known just how the dream will end.

We read in verse ten, "From ancient times the things that are not yet done." This reminds us that God is raising up some things which He spoke in the past. You are entering a season of manifestation. God has not forgotten the things He spoke to you a long time ago; they are still on His agenda. He does not forget His word. We may allow our personal word from God to become old and erode with time, but God continues to remember what He spoke to your spirit. Although it has been a long time in coming, rest assured, it shall come to pass.

## In Due Season

Transition is not always a quick work. Seasons are rarely the same length; some last longer than others. Be patient with seasons. Extract all God has for you during these times. Remember the Word of the Lord in Habakkuk 2:3, "For the vision is yet for an appointed time, but at the end it shall speak, and not lie: though it tarry, wait for it; because it will surely come, it will not tarry."

Also, take a look at the book of Job:

> *For there is hope of a tree, if it be cut down, that it will sprout again, and that the tender branch thereof will not cease. Though the root thereof wax old in the earth, and the stock thereof die in the ground; Yet through the scent of water it will bud, and bring forth boughs like a plant* (Job 14:7-9).

Job could easily be speaking of a promise or word from God that has been a long time in the soil of your spirit. In due season, it will come forth. You have treasures locked in the depths of your being that are waiting for their appointed time of manifestation.

When the Lord stated in Isaiah 46:10, “My counsel shall stand,” it affirms that God has not given up on His plan for your life. Although storms and circumstances take their toll and you might want to give up, God is staying with His plan. His Word is still out front creating the desired result. Your responsibility is to stay in the process. DON’T LET YOUR PAST DICTATE YOUR FUTURE!

# CHAPTER 3

DURING TRANSITION REMEMBER...

## SEASONS OF STRUGGLE & TESTING WILL APPEAR WITHOUT WARNING

The Bible speaks of Joseph and his dreams, with specificity to the process and its design for his life. Joseph was a man who was in transition for his entire life. Don't let that discourage you. God used Joseph in a profound way to secure the future of His people. Transition often reveals the significance of your destiny.

> *He sent a man before them, even Joseph, who was sold for a servant: Whose feet they hurt with fetters: he was laid in iron: Until the time that his word came: the word of the LORD tried him* (Psalms 105:17-19).

The word *tried* means "to refine." Until the time that Joseph's dream came to pass the commandment or dream of the Lord tried him, refined him, and improved him. The process of refinement was not destructive to Joseph, but released and improved qualities in his life that brought him to the manifestation of his dream. Transition often is a time of refinement. Fine-tuning and improving will produce a better equipped and more focused life. Be ruthless with distractions; they erode the sharpness of the dream.

### Winter Cometh

Understand the transition you are walking through is a series of seasons that prepare you to live the dream that now lives only in the corridors of your mind. Your winter season is not a punishment, but merely preparation for God's ultimate plan for your life. Get excited about your ultimate destiny. Transition is the vehicle to get you to the ultimate goal.

Transition often produces difficult seasons. There will be a season of isolation. We often call the season of isolation a "wilderness" season. Remember, the wilderness experience of Israel was because of rebellion. Maybe your season of isolation is not due to rebellion. It might be better defined as a "winter" season, not a "wilderness" season.

There are certain crops that rest dormant during a winter season. To look at them, you would think they were dead and useless. But at the first hint of spring, they awaken to new life and release the maximum harvest they were designed to release.

Your winter season is a time when you are dormant; to all outward appearances, life is about over. However, you are waiting on the first breath of spring that awakens all the promises of God inside you and brings them to fruition. Don't despise the winter season; walk through it as you now know that God is processing His greatness in you.

## Looking Within

Joseph was in this process throughout his life. You are always growing, and developing, qualities that better fit you for service in kingdom work. The refining process is present to discover, uncover, and develop qualities necessary to the vision God put in your spirit. Everything you need for the dream to materialize is within you. Too often we look outside ourselves and blame others for what has happened in our lives; we also look for others to give us a "leg up." We want to make a connection to facilitate what God has spoken to us.

Look within and discover the seeds of greatness that have been present from your birth. Even though these seeds have not been celebrated by others, they are still available to bring you from where you are—to where your dream defines that you should be. Find out what's already inside you. Those qualities become your fuel during transition. As you uncover those qualities, observe them with confidence. You are not junk. You are wonderfully and fearfully made. You are more than capable to do everything God has put in your heart.

Begin to develop the tools that will work to bring the dream to completion. The tools inside you bear the DNA of the dream God spoke to you. It's an exact match; there is a miracle inside you. Focus on the release of kingdom principles, and enjoy the greatest life you've ever known.

# CHAPTER 4

DURING TRANSITION REMEMBER...

## YOUR DREAM WILL ATTRACT FAVOR & WARFARE

> *Now Israel loved Joseph more than all his children, because he was the son of his old age: and he made him a coat of many colours. And when his brethren saw that their father loved him more than all his brethren, they hated him, and could not speak peaceably unto him* (Genesis 37:3-4).

Early in life Joseph's father gave him a coat of many colors. The gift of the coat, along with the knowledge that Joseph dreamed dreams, provoked hatred among his brothers. There were two reasons for that hatred. First, the brothers hated him because the favor of their father was on him. Joseph had gifts from the father the brothers did not enjoy. All along your journey your Father God will favor you with gifts and other blessings that will provoke dislike from others. Transition will often reveal qualities in others that disqualify them for relationship.

When the favor of the Father is on you, things happen in your life that surprise others and sometimes reveal jealousies unknown before. The dream you carry draws the favor of your Heavenly Father. His attention is constantly toward you providing every resource needed to bring to pass the vision living within. It has been said, "Favor ain't fair." When favor is present, there is an advantage in your life that others may not experience.

The second reason the brothers hated Joseph was that he was a dreamer. They hated him because of his dreams. The Bible describes the two dreams Joseph received from God. The first is found in Genesis 37:7.

> *For, behold, we were binding sheaves in the field, and, lo, my sheaf arose, and also stood upright; and, behold, your sheaves stood round about, and made obeisance to my sheaf.*

## Behold the Dreamer

Following that, the second dream is described, "And he dreamed yet another dream, and told it his brethren, and said, Behold, I have dreamed a dream more; and, behold, the sun and the moon and the eleven stars made obeisance to me" (Genesis 37:9).

Here we find two important issues about dreams. One dream was about sheaves of wheat. It has to do with the earth and earthly items. The other dream had to do with the sun and the moon and eleven stars which have to do with the heavens and heavenly items.

It is vital to know that your dream will have two edges or two sides. One part has to do with heavenly or spiritual things, and the other part of your dream has to do with the earth and natural things.

There are two sides to Jesus. One is the Person of Christ, which is the relationship side. That's what begins developing when we come to Him as our Savior. Church services often emphasize the relationship side of Christianity. It's the "touchy-feely" side of the gospel. You might say that it's the warm and fuzzy part of knowing Jesus.

The other side of Jesus is the principles He taught. Herein is where most folks will fail in the development of their vision. We get so caught up in loving Him that we don't follow His instruction.

## The Principle Thing

The principles are instructions given that produce a desired result. Like a child who climbs into the lap of a parent to say, "I love you," and the parent says, "I want you to go clean your room." The child again says, "I love you." The parent repeats, "I know you love me, but I want you to clean your room." Again the child cuddles up close, gives a big hug and says again, "I love you so much." The parent repeats the instruction once again, "I want you to clean your room."

It's wonderful to love the Lord, and develop our relationship with Him, but there is a "doing" side to every vision. It's this "doing" side that is sometimes neglected. Often it's the fear of failure and we think if we love the Lord long enough He will do the work for us. All the time God is waiting on us to discern the time, take the necessary step of obedience, and know He is with us every step of the journey.

The dreamer always makes the realist uncomfortable. The dreamer makes the religious person withdraw from fellowship. Just remember, nothing should steal your dream and you always have a God connection that will guide you through each challenge and bring you to the completion of your God assignment. Transition is always shining a light on your journey that reveals information which causes you to make choices that adjust your journey to a more precise and focused direction.

Your dream is pulling you toward a desired future. That pull will make some folks uncomfortable. Get used to it. Be energized with the spiritual revelation that God has provided to carve out the road to your future. Don't expect everyone to understand. Place your spiritual ear to the mouth of God and hear every word He speaks.

Remember, the two reasons Joseph met the hatred of his brothers were: first, he enjoyed the favor of the father and second, he was a dreamer. Notice how God kept him through a maze of situations; each of which could have destroyed him, but he stayed faithful to what he saw and remained strong and finished his God assignment.

# CHAPTER 5

DURING TRANSITION REMEMBER...

## IT'S JUST A COAT!

Joseph begins his process in Genesis 30:24, "And she called his name Joseph; and said, The LORD shall add to me another son." The name *Joseph* means "to add," which prophetically speaks of another son yet to be born. Benjamin was the second child later born to Rachel.

It is so important to know that your dream was already in you when God placed you in your mother's womb; it will take a lifetime to develop and manifest. God knew you before your mother and father knew you. He speaks this truth with clarity regarding the birth of Jeremiah:

> *Then the word of the LORD came unto me, saying, Before I formed thee in the*

> *belly I knew thee; and before thou camest forth out of the womb I sanctified thee, and I ordained thee a prophet unto the nations. Then said I, Ah, Lord GOD! behold, I cannot speak: for I am a child. But the LORD said unto me, Say not, I am a child: for thou shalt go to all that I shall send thee, and whatsoever I command thee thou shalt speak. Be not afraid of their faces: for I am with thee to deliver thee, saith the LORD* (Jeremiah 1:4-8).

God speaks from an all-knowing perspective. God is not all-thinking; He is all-knowing. He does not assimilate knowledge as time passes. He's not smarter today than He was yesterday, or last year. He is omniscient, all-knowing.

What is in your spirit today was already in you when you were born. God is not improvising and thinking it up as you move through life. He has "declared the end from the beginning." The spiritual DNA you possess will develop through many seasons to become all God desires for you. God has not only declared the end, He is standing at the end pulling you toward Himself. He's already been where you are going!

> *Now Israel loved Joseph more than all his children, because he was the son of his old age: and he made him a coat of many colours. And when his brethren saw that their father loved him more than all his brethren, they hated him,*

*and could not speak peaceably unto him* (Genesis 37:3-4).

The relationship of Joseph to his brothers decayed as Joseph shared his dreams. Quite simply, they hated him. Surely at this point he knows he is part of a dysfunctional family. Joseph now faces the challenge, or choice, to stay with the dysfunctional part of his family or to follow his dream. Tough choices are ahead.

Sometimes, transition will reveal dysfunctional areas of life that need to be adjusted or detached. These areas might have served you well for an extended period of time, but are no longer useful for the present season. They must be changed, modified, or eliminated.

While walking out the process of bringing your dream to reality you will face many tough decisions. Everyone will not celebrate what God has placed in your spirit. Often those closest to you will serve to discourage or distract you from your assignment. You must resolve to stay the course and walk to the completion of the process. Enjoy the journey and "smell the flowers" along the way.

God has already been where you are going. He is, "Declaring the end from the beginning, and from ancient times the things that are not yet done, saying, My counsel shall stand, and I will do all my pleasure" (Isaiah 46:10). Along the journey God has "handfuls on purpose" awaiting your arrival. The only way to enjoy provision for your vision is to keep moving forward. Since God has already been where you are going, He knows the way, and He is prepared to lead you the entire journey.

An interesting event takes place as Joseph meets his brothers. They take his coat and put him in a pit. Look at how this Bible text reads:

> *And it came to pass, when Joseph was come unto his brethren, that they stript Joseph out of his coat, his coat of many colours that was on him; And they took him, and cast him into a pit: and the pit was empty, there was no water in it. And they sat down to eat bread: and they lifted up their eyes and looked, and, behold, a company of Ishmeelites came from Gilead with their camels bearing spicery and balm and myrrh, going to carry it down to Egypt. And Judah said unto his brethren, What profit is it if we slay our brother, and conceal his blood? Come, and let us sell him to the Ishmeelites, and let not our hand be upon him; for he is our brother and our flesh. And his brethren were content. Then there passed by Midianites merchantmen; and they drew and lifted up Joseph out of the pit, and sold Joseph to the Ishmeelites for twenty pieces of silver: and they brought Joseph into Egypt* (Genesis 37:23-28).

First, they strip him of his coat. That coat represents the favor of the father. There may be some seasons of loss. Some will try to destroy the favor of God in your life by closing off opportunities and placing obstacles in your way. Their goal is to break your focus and keep you from completing the process which enables you to carry out your dream. It's imperative to stay in the process, don't abort the plan of God.

One thing that stands out strong in this first part of the text is that Joseph didn't fight to keep the coat. I suppose I would have fought like crazy to keep what represented the favor of the father in my life. To fight for the coat would have become a distraction in the life of Joseph. To fight for the coat would have meant he did not keep the main thing as the main thing. The main thing here was the dream, not the coat.

# CHAPTER 6

DURING TRANSITION REMEMBER...

## LEARN WHEN TO HOLD 'EM & WHEN TO FOLD 'EM

It's also important to know when to fight and when to let go. Too often we fight for things we should be releasing. When things have served their season in our life, it's time to let them go. The difficult part is to know when to "hold 'em" and when to "fold 'em." To get involved in a fight that doesn't belong to you is simply a distraction and keeps you from moving on in the process of God.

Transition provides for constant decision making. You can't go into a cave and hope everything will disappear. It will rarely disappear; it will mostly get bigger and more complex. You will need to ask God to help you make quality decisions and make them often.

Just a brief illustration fits right here. We can look at David when he is at the point of decision that will bring him into a direct confrontation with Goliath. When David meets his brothers at the site of the confrontation one of the first questions he asks is, "What will be given the man who defeats this giant?" The answer came:

> *And the men of Israel said, Have ye seen this man that is come up? surely to defy Israel is he come up: and it shall be, that the man who killeth him, the king will enrich him with great riches, and will give him his daughter, and make his father's house free in Israel* (1 Samuel 17:25).

It seems as though David is deciding whether fighting this giant is worth the trouble. Apparently there is an option. He can fight or he can walk away. Obviously, to fight would be the manly thing to do at this point. However, to walk away, even though it would seem cowardly, might not be a bad decision. How does he go about making the decision, and what facts are considered before the final word is given?

## The Anointing Abides

Before we take this too far, I want you to remember what had happened in an earlier chapter of 1 Samuel. This is a part we often forget when we talk of David and Goliath. 1 Samuel 16:13 says, "Then Samuel took the horn of oil, and anointed him in the midst of his brethren: and the Spirit of the LORD came upon David from that day forward." Samuel anointed David to be King. Although Saul was still reigning, David was the one on whom the Spirit of the Lord rested.

Transition will always provide an anointing for the season in which you walk. The anointing will precede the season; therefore, when you enter the season, you will already carry the anointing that will transition you through that particular season. You might also receive an anointing that will manifest quite some time before a season appears. Rest assured, God would always provide resources, which enable you to transition through each season.

### Fighting the Good Fight

Now, back to our original story of David and Goliath. David is deciding whether or not to fight Goliath. He does learn the prize for killing this giant is three-fold: the first thing is the one who kills Goliath will receive great riches. So far that means it's David's fight. The second prize was the one who kills Goliath would receive the king's daughter in marriage. Last of all, the family of the one killing Goliath would be free from taxes.

Well, all that sounds pretty good. I think David believes it's his fight to fight and win. However, which of the three do you think was the clincher that really let David know it was his fight and he should not walk away?

Let's alleviate the suspense. David's focus was on the prize of receiving the king's daughter in marriage! That's not so bad. It had very little to do with the beauty of the king's daughter. David, who had been anointed king, was keenly aware that kings marry princesses! The king's daughter was the princess, and it was a match made by God to bring David out of obscurity and into his destiny.

Therefore, David knew it was his fight for ANYTHING THAT STANDS BETWEEN YOU AND YOUR DESTINY BECOMES YOUR FIGHT! ANYTHING ELSE IS SIMPLY A DISTRACTION! The throne was his destiny and Goliath stood between where David was and a wedding that could cause a kingly recognition to come from others.

Now, let's get back to Joseph and his dream. He's losing a coat and has to decide whether to fight for the coat or let it go. How do you know when to fight and when to let go? To keep it simple, you fight for something when it is directly related to your dream and destiny. Anything else, you can let go or negotiate.

That coat was not directly related to the dream and destiny of Joseph. It was not worth fighting over. Joseph didn't need a coat to know he had the favor of the father in his life. When you lose some things in your life never let that loss negate the favor of God in your life.

When circumstances come into your life that are in opposition to your dream, you must reach deep within your heart to access the resources needed to stay the course and complete the journey. Remember, all you need is already within you. Find it, activate it, and use it. God is in you working His plan.

# CHAPTER 7

DURING TRANSITION REMEMBER...

## SOMETIMES LIFE'S JUST THE PITS!

Now, Joseph is hated by his brothers, he has lost his coat, and before he can turn around twice, he finds himself in a pit. Life just isn't getting any better for the "dreamer."

As we mentioned before, your dream will often produce seasons of loneliness and isolation. Joseph was alone in the pit. I'm sure in that pit there was time for contemplation of whether he would survive and go on to complete the dream, or whether this was the end of the journey and the dream was just a fantasy and would never be realized.

While your enemy wants to destroy your dream, you must never forget that he also wants to destroy you. The fight is against the dream and the dreamer. If the enemy can destroy the dreamer, the dream dies. If the enemy destroys the dream, the dreamer lives a life of death on the inside and never knows the accomplishment God intended.

This has a direct correlation with a "mom-to-be" carrying the life of her child in her womb. If something happens to the child, the expecting mother has to live with many conflicting emotions. What if? How? Why? Will I ever have the child of promise? Something in her dies even though she still walks and talks. There is a void that can never be adequately filled. Should something happen to the mom-to-be, the unborn child oft-times dies without having the benefit of knowing life outside the womb. Both situations are tragic. Both situations reflect a tremendous loss.

Transition can provide mixed emotions, and distorted perceptions about life and the future. When we live out of our spirit-man those mixed emotions and distorted perceptions are brought into the spirit realm, where they can be felt and seen clearly without distortion.

While carrying your unborn dream, it is imperative that you take care of your personal spiritual nourishment. I know it's important to prepare for the dream to come to manifestation; but it is equally, if not more important, to keep yourself spiritually healthy so that your inner dream can receive nourishment from the intake of spiritual food coming into your life.

## Getting Out of the Pit

There are some things that pertain to your dream only you can provide. These are times when you feel loneliness and isolation with intensity. No one else can help. You have to feel your way along an uncertain path. I encourage you to keep going and believe God for favor. Your dream is destined to manifest and you will live and not die.

As Joseph sat in the pit, I'm sure one of the thoughts that entered his mind is, 'This can't be where I die; I didn't see this in the dream. I'm just in the pits. It must be a temporary setback. I refuse to give it more than what it deserves.' Some days you just find yourself in the pits! "Well, I'm in the pits," you say. Now, how can I get out of the pits? Here's how to get out of the pits. When Joseph was in the pits it was Judah who came to take him out of the pit. *Judah* means PRAISE!

Praise will always get you out of the pits. When things go wrong and you enter seasons you didn't see in the dream, please remember that praise will change your environment in a heartbeat. Keep living out of your spirit-man, and you will not give in to natural human emotions.

# CHAPTER 8

DURING TRANSITION REMEMBER...

## GOD TURNS MISTAKES INTO MIRACLES

The choices Joseph made ultimately brought him into a pit. I suppose you could say that Joseph made some mistakes by telling his brothers his dream, not once, but twice. Well, I realize that sometimes we do make mistakes. We often make choices that are not so wise, and those choices can cause some pain and discomfort.

During transition, you are always in position for God to manifest a miracle to facilitate the exit of one season and the entrance to another season. Joseph gets out of the pit via the persuasiveness of Judah, but is sold to a band of Ishmaelites. It's a bit strange that Joseph is sold to a group of folks that descended from Abraham's mistake. It was Abraham's son, Ishmael, which was born before Isaac that caused pain in the life of Abraham. Now, the descendants of Ishmael are transporting Joseph to Egypt. Life gets even crazier for him.

Keep in mind that today's Ishmael can deliver tomorrow's promise. In a circumstance that seems to have no resolution, God always provides a way of escape. The King always has one more move. God is never surprised at your circumstance. He is never taken off guard by what enters your life. God's not nervous, nor hyper; He's always at peace and in control.

During transition, things often seem to be a bit crazy. Days and weeks of unexplainable events and circumstances enter and exit your life. You will think you live in a perpetual need for a miracle. Life seems to be lived on the edge of destruction. Any moment could be the moment life disappears. During these times it's good to remember that circumstances often scream the opposite of "truth." Truth is what God has spoken, not what circumstances are screaming.

### Receiving A Miracle

Even when you make choices that are not so favorable to your journey, you can rest in the knowledge that God can turn any mistake into a miracle. You are moments from that desired miracle every step of your journey. Remain alert and expectant. Certain qualities must be present in your heart and mind to receive these miracles that come during transition. There must be a positive, faith-filled, and expectant attitude throughout any season of transition. Some of the qualities that must remain present in your life are:

IN TRANSITION...You need to identify the miracle needed. You might not like where you are, but you cannot change your condition without a change in your position or mindset. Decide where you want to be, then your miracle has an open door into your life.

IN TRANSITION...Select passages from God's Word which confirm God's opinion that you should have your miracle. His Word must be the foundation of all transitional journeys.

IN TRANSITION...Be confident and ask God for your miracle. Never assume that because He knows what you need that there is no need to be specific and ask for that miracle.

IN TRANSITION...Hang around folks who trust God for their own miracles. Remember, God created you to climb, not cower. He made you to fly, not fail.

IN TRANSITION...Be sure to speak a positive outcome. Let others hear your expectant conversation. Never speak about your doubts. Your conversation will always reveal to others the direction your life is moving. Be clear and be articulate about your future.

IN TRANSITION...See your vision as complete. Abraham saw stars and visualized children; a woman visualized a touch of the hem of His garment and saw healing. Jesus saw the resurrection and ascension, not the cross and the grave. "For the joy that was set before Him, endured the cross" (Hebrews 12:2).

IN TRANSITION...Never let go in the hours of darkness what God promised in the illumination of His Word. Miracles are for the unrelenting, not the wisher. Reach for your miracle.

During transition, God turns mistakes into miracles. Anticipate them, position yourself to receive them, make room for them, and celebrate their arrival! It's your "DUE SEASON!"

# CHAPTER 9

DURING TRANSITION REMEMBER...

## YOU HAVE TO LEARN TO LAUGH & ASK, "ARE WE THERE YET?"

As a small boy, about once each year, my family and I would take a trip to visit relatives. When mom and dad would tell me about the trip, excitement would build to a fever pitch. Each day I would ask a few questions about the trip; mom would take her time as she provided answers. Her answers always produced another level of excitement and expectation in my mind.

Finally, the day would come when we were to depart. The car would be packed, and I always brought a few things with me to occupy my time during the journey. As we would drive away from our house and begin the long trip to see family, which we had not seen in quite some time, my mind would pre-play the fun I would have when we arrived. It didn't matter what I brought to occupy my time or how many games I played along the way, shortly after departing I would always ask the question, "Are we there yet?" It would be followed by another similar, question, "How long do we have before we get there?"

I had the promise of a wonderful time, but the promise seemed like it would never come to pass. I would grow tired of the trip and often would be overcome with anxiety and frustration while waiting for us to get to the promised destination.

There is a great parallel here as we think of a promise God gave us some time ago and the excitement and expectation the promise provided. However, during the time between the promise and the manifestation, anxiety and frustration often arise, and we become so impatient that we think it will never manifest.

Human nature hasn't changed in several hundred years. Abraham had the same problem. God gave him a promise and years came and went and the promise didn't manifest. Abraham grew weary in believing. God would often visit him and renew the promise. Abraham grew so tired of Him renewing the promise, that when God appeared one time later in Abraham's life, his reaction was to laugh at God.

Take a look at the account in the book of Genesis:

> *And God said unto Abraham, As for Sarai thy wife, thou shalt not call her name Sarai, but Sarah shall her name be. And I will bless her, and give thee a son also of her: yea, I will bless her, and she shall be a mother of nations; kings of people shall be of her. Then Abraham fell upon his face, and laughed, and said in his heart, Shall a child be born unto him that is an hundred years old? and shall Sarah, that is ninety years old, bear?* (Genesis 17:15-17).

Hey, not only did Abraham laugh at the promise of God, Sarah had a similar reaction. Take a look:

> *And they said unto him, Where is Sarah thy wife? And he said, Behold, in the tent. And he said, I will certainly return unto thee according to the time of life; and, lo, Sarah thy wife shall have a son. And Sarah heard it in the tent door, which was behind him. Now Abraham and Sarah were old and well stricken in age; and it ceased to be with Sarah after the manner of women. Therefore Sarah laughed within herself, saying, After I am waxed old shall I have pleasure, my lord being old also? And the LORD said unto Abraham, Wherefore did Sarah laugh, saying, Shall I of a surety bear a child, which am old? Is any thing too*

> *hard for the LORD? At the time appointed I will return unto thee, according to the time of life, and Sarah shall have a son* (Genesis 18:9-14).

The issue Abraham and Sarah faced was that the promise God was making to them seemed to be so far removed from their present circumstance that it was ridiculous to think it would ever come to pass. However, we must remember that God said there is nothing too hard for Him. If God said it, then it's not a matter of "if it will happen," it's only a matter of "when will it happen?"

When you have a big dream, your faith must explode at another level. The laughter of Abraham and Sarah did not change God's Word, but they did have to take God seriously. In response, God began to move with the manifestation of the promise.

I've seen days of prolonged craziness that were so ridiculous that I actually had a deep resounding time of laughter as I was going through the crazy stuff. To me, it all seemed unreal.

There are moments when God speaks a future which seems so far removed from where you are presently living that you wonder if you will ever reach the destination. During transition, when you face frustrating times in which you are tempted to yield to anxiety; you must remember: **THERE IS NOTHING TOO HARD FOR GOD!**

In answer to the question, "Are we there yet?" The answer is, "Maybe not just yet, but we will get there because God said we would!" Now, take a moment and laugh at the enemy who thinks you can be kept from the manifestation of what God promised.

# CHAPTER 10

DURING TRANSITION REMEMBER...

## CHARACTER IS VERY IMPORTANT

Joseph gets to Egypt and finds favor. Potiphar buys Joseph from the Ishmaelites and makes him overseer of his house. God blesses the house for the sake of Joseph. However, Potiphar's wife has eyes for Joseph and tries to entice him to lie with her, but Joseph refuses. He is accused of a moral failure by Potiphar's wife, and Joseph finds himself in prison.

Even in prison, Joseph rises to the level of leadership. This man is in transition most of his life but he continues to rise to the top in every situation. His character has become the guiding force of his decision-making.

During times of transition you can be tempted to take a short cut to get to the destination you desire. You might be asked to do or say things which will compromise principles by which you have chosen to live. It's important to remember that **character**, not **charisma**, is the most important quality to manifest during transition.

Charisma attracts, but character sustains. Character embodies who you really are at the core. It's the inner fiber of your being. It's your inner self in action. It reveals what you are truly made of; it's your inner substance. If you manifest charisma without character, it's only a matter of time before people discover your real self. Without character you cannot sustain meaningful relationships, and without relationships your ability to process through seasons of transition is anemic. So, what is it about character that really makes a difference?

## Character Creates Trust

Influence functions on the basis of trust. If you pull out trust, you will lose your focus in transition.

Joseph was a person of influence in the house of Potiphar because Potiphar could trust Joseph. Although this was a season of transition, Joseph functioned as a man of character, and that quality provided promotion and increase in his life.

## Character Promotes Excellence

Good character sets a standard for everyone you influence. Character in transition provides a foundation for favor to move into your life.

Excellence was found throughout the life of Joseph. Excellence was a quality of life which became a magnet for the favor of strategic relationships to enter his life. The larger picture was that Joseph was in transition through Potiphar's house; he was destined for Pharaoh's house.

## Character Gives Staying Power

During the tough days of transition, its character that provides strength to carry you the final distance to your dream. Even when you are inclined to quit, character will keep you going.

Staying power was manifested in the life of Joseph as he remained true to his inner convictions during difficult times, even times of false accusations. It was the "staying power" of character that enabled him to function under great adversity.

## Character Will Determine Your Legacy

Your gifts and determination might dictate your potential, but it's your character that will determine your legacy. The day could come when progress seems to call for a compromise of conviction. Part of you will want to push forward; after all, you've come so far. The end justifies the means. But there will be another voice as well. The message will be simple, short, and without explanation: "This is wrong."

Character is vital to the accomplishment of your dream and the fulfillment of your God assignment. In a day when so many are taking short cuts to keep up with the perceived "front runners" in Christianity, it's important to remember the significance of character.

If character can create trust, promote excellence, give staying power, and determine your legacy, then it's a "must" ingredient to manifest in your life at a high level. There seems to be no adequate substitute found for good character. No imitation and no replacement can be set up. Settle for no less than the highest quality of character to be manifested during each transitional season.

# CHAPTER 11

DURING TRANSITION REMEMBER...

## YOU MUST DISCERN RELATIONSHIPS IN YOUR LIFE

While in charge of the prison, Joseph comes in contact with the chief butler and the chief baker of Pharaoh's house. They had displeased the king and found themselves in prison with Joseph. One morning they came before Joseph looking sad and Joseph asked the reason for their sadness. They told Joseph of a dream they had dreamed, and they were sad because no one could tell them the meaning of the dream.

Joseph is a dreamer as well as an interpreter of dreams. Remember, Joseph had dreams and told the meaning of his dreams to his brothers who promptly put him in a pit. It was the interpreting of dreams that had provided more than enough trouble for Joseph. It seemed that for each season of transition that involved dreams, Joseph would endure additional pain. Now, he has to decide if he will interpret the dream of the butler and the baker.

After listening to the dreams, the interpretation is that the butler would be restored to his position in three days, but the baker would lose his life in three days without any restoration. Joseph asks the butler to remember him when he is restored; he has nothing more to say to the baker.

During transition, you might need to disconnect from some relationships that are taking you nowhere. Joseph disconnected from the baker. The baker was going nowhere. Any relationship with the baker was a dead end. No pun intended!

Transition offers a time when you must discern relationships and their proper place in your life. Some relationships are temporary, while others are long term. It's your job to discern who falls into which category.

Joseph perceived his brothers would not be with him through transitional times in his life. They never understood his dreams, nor were they willing to tolerate hearing about them on a regular basis. In fact, quite a few people entered, and exited the life of Joseph as he transitioned from place to place. Real issues would have developed had Joseph tried to keep all these relationships with him throughout the entire journey of his life. Some detached early, but joined him again later.

The discerning of relationships is a key to successful transition. God has assigned people to connect with you for different parts of the journey. There is mutual blessing as those relationships are nurtured. It's important to remember that God not only has folks join your journey, but also equally important is the fact that you will join others along the way. Others will be a blessing to you as you are a blessing to them. Some are assigned to you while you are assigned to others.

## Managing Your Alone Time

As relationships ebb and flow in your life, it's good to remember there will be some "alone time." How you mange this alone time will certainly help navigate your life during transition. Some activities you might want to try as you deal with relationships along the way are:

- Never allow "alone time" to feel like a prison. Create a sanctuary during moments when relationships seem far away. Even Abraham and Lot had to separate.

- When folks you've walked with for quite some time decide to exit your life, refuse to allow a spirit of grief to enter your heart. Take a moment and create a place and time for worship.

Turn your attention toward your Heavenly Father. He is your ultimate source.

- Be willing to break a soul-tie from prior seasons of your life. Great pain comes when we try to hold on to a soul-tie whose season is completed. It's always difficult to break soul-ties. The familiar is always more comfortable. Even the children of Israel spoke of returning to Egypt because they knew that even a bad environment could be more comfortable.

- Also, during the shifting of relationships, be alert to divine appointments. The butler and the baker were divine appointments for Joseph when he was at a very low point in his life.

God will never fail to bring people across your path that will help you transition to your next level. You cannot manipulate the will of God. Just keep doing what you know to do; run with your passion, and God will do the rest. There will always be folks who will promise you the stars and moon but they will seldom deliver. Let God bring the people into your life who will celebrate your God assignment.

Transition is a time to hold on to some relationships and let go of others. God is now maneuvering His Kingdom folks, getting them into position for the greatest harvest the world has ever seen. You are one of them.

# CHAPTER 12

DURING TRANSITION REMEMBER...

## GOD RESTORES EVERYTHING THAT HAS BEEN LOST

Transition seems to be a series of seasons in which we suffer loss. It's hard to realize blessing and prosperity during most transitions. However, transition provides moments of miracles that reinforce our belief system and bring us to a closer relationship with the God who is more than enough.

Miracles in the life of Joseph were many. From his brothers decision to spare his life, his deliverance from the pit, his journey to Egypt, the false accusations, his imprisonment, and even his being forgotten by the butler when he was restored. Joseph experienced "handfuls on purpose" along his journey. At each place of pain, there was a promise, and there was a way through to the next level.

If we only look at what Joseph lost, the story would be very sad. When we look at the miracles we understand the overriding presence of God that dominated each circumstance and provided all Joseph needed during transition.

**Restoration Principles**

I have found that God restores, or compensates, for what we perceive as loss. Let's take four areas of God's restoration that have stood with me for almost fifty years.

During times of pressure and circumstances which challenge and stretch your thinking, you often come to the place when it's very difficult to make a decision. When the last few decisions that have been made have produced even tougher times, you get to the place you don't want to make any decision for fear of it following the same pattern of pain. Emotions become unstable and nothing in life seems to be dependable; it's difficult to continue moving forward. We sometimes decide to go into an emotional cave and wait for the storm to pass.

Joseph must have had moments when he wondered if he could ever have a clear thought again. In the pit and in prison, the years of obscurity take their toll on Joseph's dream. I'm sure he questioned his own ability to process information during these times of transition.

King David found this out during some dark days in his own life. He had transition times as well. David had some of the same things happen in his life that have happened in the lives of others. He couldn't even trust his own decision-making, and clear thinking seemed far away until he reconnected with God.

Then he could say, "He restoreth my soul" (Psalms 23:3). David found that God could restore his ability to think clearly and make quality decisions again. God will do the same for you. David's soul was restored; peace returned to his mind. He could have good thoughts again...peaceful thoughts.

## God's Provision

Often during transition times, our physical body breaks down. The uncommon pressure and effort it takes to process through some of these seasons causes an open door for the enemy to attack us physically. It could happen to us, or to one of our loved ones. Regardless, it becomes a battle that must be fought and won. God provides encouragement for this life experience as well.

God says, through Jeremiah the prophet, "For I will restore health unto thee" (Jeremiah 30:17). Healing is yours through the stripes Jesus bore on Calvary's cross. Basic provision for the body is available continually for everyone. Transition does not abdicate the promise of God. You still have full rights and privileges in Him.

Another price that is often paid during transition is that we lose our joy. Once we were eager to participate, now we seem like a robot. Someone winds us up, we go and perform, then return to the box awaiting another wind up and send out. Participation is no longer fun. We dread the times when we are asked to participate. It all seems so inconvenient. We would rather be left alone.

Joseph must have had times when joy seemed so far away. I'm sure there were other times when he would have let the dream go during persecution and betrayal and even when folks lied to him. He had people lie to him and lie about him. That had to remove some of his eagerness to participate in his own future.

God has a word for those who have lost their joy, "Restore unto me the joy of thy salvation" (Psalms 51:12). God would never leave you without joy. It's the joy of the Lord that is your strength. God will restore your eagerness to participate. It's coming back. Look for that day when your joy is restored. You will enjoy participating in your assignment again. The process of transition will, once again, be a joyous challenge that you meet and celebrate.

## God Restores Time

Transition also seems to use time. Time is a commodity that we always lose, and rarely gain. From my personal experience, I have felt more loss of time during transition than anything else. How will I ever get back "time" that I've lost? When I stop to think about time that's been wasted, I get sad. I often wonder if there is enough time left in life to accomplish what is in my heart. Time, time, time... there just doesn't seem to be enough!

God said, through the prophet, "And I will restore to you the years that the locust hath eaten" (Joel 2:25). How incredible! God will give back time that has been unused.

I believe Joseph felt that time had been lost through the years of transition. It seemed impossible it could ever be brought back. However, God has a way of working it out for His glory. Time ultimately became the friend of Joseph.

Please know that God will restore everything needed for the seasons of transition as well as provide for the entire journey of life.

# CHAPTER 13

DURING TRANSITION REMEMBER...

## YOUR JOURNEY INVOLVES SOLVING BIG PROBLEMS FOR OTHERS

Some time after the butler was released from prison he was serving Pharaoh, and he learned that Pharaoh had a dream. Pharaoh had called all the wise men of the kingdom to see if he could find the meaning of the dream. No one could interpret the dream; everyone was frustrated. The butler remembered how Joseph had provided the meaning of the butler's dream some years ago.

Now, the real problem is, how do you tell Pharaoh that the man who can provide the meaning of his dream is in jail. Not only in jail, but a convicted rapist! The butler has a real dilemma on his hands. However, he finally tells Pharaoh about Joseph, and Pharaoh asked for Joseph to come before him.

Joseph is summoned and starts the process of moving from the prison to the palace. In my mind, I have Joseph still in jail clothes, moving through the prison doors, out into the courtyard and toward the palace to meet the most powerful man in the world. I also believe that the important people of Pharaoh's realm were all around watching Joseph on his long walk to stand before Pharaoh and deal with the dream.

Somewhere in the process of the journey, I'm pretty sure he sees Potiphar and his wife. Remember, it was Potiphar's wife who falsely accused Joseph of raping her. As their eyes lock on each other, Joseph must have had a million thoughts race through his mind. Could this be his big chance for pay back? Maybe this is his time for vengeance for the false accusation leveled against his life. No, Joseph, a man of character and deep core values, moves his attention from Potiphar and his wife, and continues on his walk to Pharaoh's court.

Right here is a great lesson for those in transition. At some point in transition you will have to get over some Potiphar spirits that have done you wrong. You have to bypass the opportunity to extract vengeance and move on to your ultimate destiny. Your future is more important than spending time on those who refuse to celebrate your journey. Your future is brighter than any yesterday. Remain focused on where God is leading you, never on the pain of the past. Transition is a time of movement, so keep moving—moving toward the ultimate destiny God has prepared.

### Problem Solver

Now, Joseph gets to Pharaoh and interprets his dream. There will be seven years of plenty to be followed by seven years of famine. Joseph exhorts Pharaoh to find a man who can lead and set him as the one in charge of gathering up food during the seven years of plenty. Joseph's conversation with Pharaoh included more than just giving the meaning of the dream. Joseph brought a solution to Pharaoh. Therefore, Joseph was not made prime minister of Egypt because he interpreted dreams; he was made prime minister because he solved a national crisis.

Sometime during transition, you will have an opportunity for a God-connection that will solve a major problem for someone else. Look for that moment; it could be your moment of promotion. Never get so locked into transition that you fail to notice strategic moments that offer opportunities for promotion.

Your next level is a heartbeat away. Stay alert to opportunities that come before your life. There is only a brief moment you can capitalize on a window of opportunity. Don't miss that opportunity. Joseph is put over a kingdom because he is a problem-solver.

## The Three Coats of Transition

Right here I want to provide an insight to encourage you. I think it's quite amazing to follow the coats of Joseph. We know he had three coats. There's a quick lesson to be learned as we take a look at these three coats.

His father gave the first coat to Joseph, and his brothers took it. We don't know where he got the second coat; but we know he had a second coat because Potiphar's wife took it when he fled from her. The third coat appears when he interprets Pharaoh's dream, and Pharaoh puts raiment on Joseph which includes a coat that belonged to Pharaoh.

These three coats can represent three dimensions of transition. There is the 30-fold dimension of transition which is the beginning where you often lose some things. The second is the 60-fold dimension of transition when you lose some other items you thought you might need. Finally, there is the 100-fold dimension of transition when everything you've lost is restored and no one can take that from you. The King puts his coat on you and no one can take that away.

Joseph never asked for a coat, nor did he fight for a coat. He allowed the process of transition to provide coats as he needed them. However, when he needed permanence, the king gave a coat that no one could take away.

# CHAPTER 14

DURING TRANSITION REMEMBER...

## THERE IS ALWAYS A LARGER PICTURE THAN WHAT YOU PRESENTLY VIEW

Joseph only saw sheaves of wheat bowing to another sheaf of wheat. He only saw stars bowing to another star. He only saw a coat, a tiny pit, and a long journey to Egypt. He saw promotion given, and then taken away; he saw a prison and experienced friends forgetting him. He saw Pharaoh, the interpretation of a dream, and another job in Pharaoh's world. These were only small photographs of a much larger picture.

If we were to go back in time many years before Joseph's story appears on the pages of God's Word, we would find God talking to a man named Abram about his future. God Himself provided his transitions and the challenges of each transition. It went something like this:

> *And he said unto Abram, Know of a surety that thy seed shall be a stranger in a land that is not theirs, and shall serve them; and they shall afflict them four hundred years; And also that nation, whom they shall serve, will I judge: and afterward shall they come out with great substance* (Genesis 15:13-14).

The larger picture encompasses more than Abram and Joseph. The larger picture is that God will oversee the transition of Abram's seed throughout generations. The seed of Abram, later to be Abraham, would have as part of their transition, a trip to a land where they would serve for four hundred years. After their servitude, they would exit with great substance. Quite a promise; wouldn't you say?

It was Joseph's part of the grand picture to become the head of Egypt so that he could save food during seven years of plenty. Seven years of famine would come afterward and no one would have food except those who were in Egypt. In order to avoid famine, folks from all over the world moved to Egypt and brought everything they had to exchange for food. Even Joseph's brothers came looking for food.

It was the famine which brought the wealth of the world to Egypt so it would already be in place for the children of Israel when they were delivered from bondage; they would come out with great substance. Joseph was the instrument

God used to facilitate the exit of Abraham's seed from bondage to the land of promise.

Joseph was ultimately at a strategic point, in a window of opportunity, to be used by God to save a generation and transition them from bondage to freedom.

I can tell you right now, God is still monitoring the big picture. He has something strategic for you to accomplish. Stay with His plan, and move through seasons of transition, endure hardship, remain strong and faithful. Always exhibit godly character and be anchored to biblical core values for God will bring to manifestation what He spoke to you in the past.

You only see a small part of what God wants to accomplish. Even on the grandest scale, we only see for a generation or two. Our responsibility is to make a mark in our generation. Abraham made his mark. Isaac made his mark. Jacob made his mark. Joseph made his mark and many others made their mark. It was all done that we might be right where we presently are located—ready to hand the future to the next generation of promise.

# CHAPTER 15

DURING TRANSITION REMEMBER...

## SOMETIMES YOU NEED TO HAVE A PARTY!

There is a Scripture from which I have gained much strength during my personal transition times. I'd like to share these additional thoughts with you. God's Word records in the book of Acts these words, "For in him we live, and move, and have our being" (Acts 17:28). I believe every successful transition takes place "IN HIM." Every season of transition must have, as its foundation, a position in Christ. Any transition which does not take place in Him is doomed at the beginning.

There is an interesting phrase in this Scripture that has been preached for many years by some of the best preachers of the age. Generations have brought this to our attention; yet, I have never found it tied to a season of transition. It is, of course, "IN HIM."

In Genesis we find the account of Adam and Eve. We read that God caused a deep sleep to fall on Adam and while in that sleep God took a rib and made a woman for Adam. The biblical account uses the words, "And He closed up the flesh instead thereof" (Genesis 2:21).

Adam now has a bride who is to walk with him, keep him company, and be a part of his life. The specific wording of the closing of the flesh is interesting to me. I know it would be improper for the flesh to be left open. In fact, the closing of the flesh lets us know the work is complete.

Now, let your mind run fast forward through centuries. Jesus is hanging on the cross and a soldier takes a spear and runs it into His side. "But one of the soldiers with a spear pierced his side, and forthwith came there out blood and water" (John 19:34).

The next scene is after the resurrection. Jesus is appearing to his disciples, and Thomas is with them at this appearing. John provides this account: "Then saith he to Thomas, Reach hither thy finger, and behold my hands; and reach hither thy hand, and thrust it into my side" (John 20:27).

Putting these three accounts together we notice that the first Adam was provided a bride from his side and the flesh was closed. Jesus, the SECOND ADAM, apparently has a side that remains open after the resurrection, or the words, "thrust it into my side" would not be present. The significance of the "open side" seems to speak to the truth that the bride of the Second Adam has to re-enter before the closing can take place.

God's Word seems to bear this out as the words, "IN HIM" and "IN CHRIST" are found approximately 200 times in Scripture text. If I am, "IN HIM," it is from that location that I can "LIVE, MOVE, and HAVE BEING." Then, it might be time to HAVE A PARTY! Even during transition you can be safe from harm as you dwell in Him. There is a security in Christ that can be found no other place. We are in Him, a protected environment, and from there we can experience transition safely and without fear.

### We Can Live

The word "live" means we can be strong, fresh, and efficient. During transition it's important that we be able to remain strong for the journey. The joy of the Lord remains our strength. Joy will be an attribute we experience as we move through the seasons of transition. Strength for each day will be present when we awaken. Even when we are not aware of what the day will bring, we know that IN HIM we are more than up for the task.

What better time to experience freshness. IN HIM we realize fresh ideas, creativity, God moments, and the energy to carry out His instructions. No longer does it seem that we go around the same mountain again and again. There is a bright, clean outlook which is uncluttered with the debris of past experiences that produced pain. It all happens "IN HIM!" Transition can become a time of freshness with new horizons to view.

Besides strength and freshness, we can enjoy effectiveness. Oh my goodness, how often have we felt the reminders of yesterday's efforts which could not produce positive results? Efficiency causes us to run the race without the taxing effort of fighting every battle ourselves. The battle is the Lord's. Effectiveness produces an opportunity to celebrate moments of progress and victories throughout transition.

Whew! This reminds me of the day my wife told me we were expecting our first child. In those days we didn't know much about trimesters, sonograms, and such things. The doctor just told you a baby was on the way, and you started planning on the new arrival.

Now there are trimesters, sonograms and much more information during the early stages of pregnancy. The word "LIVE" speaks to me of the first trimester of pregnancy. You find out there is life, and it's in a safe place. You know you will care for that life and experience its growth and development. Over time, you will have a new, healthy baby. Even though there is no detected movement, you know life is present. It's precious, and you intend to lay down your own life to see its complete development. That life on the inside of the mother will go through seasons of transition before the birth actually happens, but the transition goes on in a safe environment, protected from harmful elements.

This first trimester is a season of limitation. There are personal changes that take place. Often, things in the home are rearranged, changed, or modified to accommodate that which is coming at an appropriate season. Even though there is an experience called, "morning sickness," you get through the tough times because you know what's in the future. Your limitations are not just external, but also internal. Adjustments are made in all areas of life.

So is your destiny. It's inside the womb of your spirit. You are IN HIM, a protected environment, and you are safe from harmful elements. He has laid down His life to secure a healthy birth for His purpose. There are always adjustments to be made both internal and external. You get through the tough times because you are keenly aware of the future celebration.

## We Can Move

Ahhhhh, this means we are set in motion. Wow! That's what I need to know when I'm experiencing transition. I need to know for sure that I am moving toward God's intended purpose. Often, I'm not so sure. In Him, I can be sure my movement is safe and in the proper direction.

This stage reminds me of the second trimester of carrying a baby. Now there is movement that proves the life inside is properly transitioning. We know there is development because of movement that is detected. The second trimester is a time of preparing for the new arrival. During this transition, the sickness begins to pass, and the celebration of carrying a new life becomes more enjoyable. You can hear the heartbeat and the bonding process begins. Visual changes also take place as you make a place for the baby to live.

IN HIM, our second trimester of transition represents the passing of many uncertainties. The realization that what God spoke to us is growing in us, and it is headed toward a due season of manifestation. Your energy level rises to meet the new challenges you face during this transition.

### We Can Have Our Being

To "have being" speaks of hope or expectation that what we believe will actually be manifested. Dreams do come true! The life in your recreated spirit is transitioning toward a desired end. When the Word of God says we are created in "HIS IMAGE" it doesn't mean we physically look like Him; it rather means we are created as He sees us.

Hey, quite frankly, not everyone thinks all babies are beautiful. However, you always believe your babies are beautiful. You think they are beautiful because they are born with all the beauty you expected. You expect your baby to be beautiful, successful, happy, and secure. That child is created beautifully in your eyes.

This word "being" speaks to me of the third and final trimester of pregnancy. The third trimester is the trimester of transition. This trimester is filled with discomfort from head to toe. We are all aware that nothing less than delivery will relieve the pressure caused by carrying this baby to full term.

Sometime during this season LABOR BEGINS! This is the point of chaos. When nature announces the process is completing; it seems like everything happens at once. The gathering of bags which have been pre-packed; the loading of the car; the rushing to the hospital; the calling of family members; the admitting to the hospital; the examining that determine just how far along the process has moved, and countless other thoughts that invade the mind.

Sometime during this process of labor the pain intensifies to the point of being unbearable.

Then, and only then, does the mother come to a life-defining moment called TRANSITION! At this time the baby moves into place for the final stage of delivery. As the end nears, the mother needs someone to remind her of what, in fact, she already knows. She desperately needs direction in the midst of this crisis; she needs a coach. Now, there is no turning back.

Spiritual transition is like being in labor; the promise that grows inside has to come out. There is no other option. Enduring hunger stretches you beyond the routine and comfort of your ordinary world. Change is about to manifest, but rest assured, it will come with pain. The transition of your promise begins a shifting in your life that feels like death to your own dreams and the birthing of God's.

For the mother who is having her first child, there is no point of reference for the transition she will experience. So is the birthing of God's dream for your life. Always know that God will reveal Himself in greater and mightier ways!

# CHAPTER 16

DURING TRANSITION REMEMBER...

## THERE WILL BE TRANSITION INDICATORS

> *For **in him** we live, and move, and have our being; as certain also of your own poets have said, For we are also his offspring* (Acts 17:28).

Although it seems that all transition actually takes place "IN HIM," we usually look at transition as a purely external event over a process of time. However, transition often happens both externally and internally. When one happens without the other there is anxiety, confusion, and fear. When transition happens within and without there is peace, confidence, and assurance of a desired end.

Whether or not we move forward in our vision, purpose, and growth during this transition time will largely depend upon our ability to correctly confront and navigate through some unique challenges.

The children of Israel were able to come out of Egypt, yet unable to enter into the Promised Land due to the way in which they handled the transition season.

There are three indicators, or challenges, that assist us in identifying transition. Each indicator has unique challenges. We must navigate each one with the wisdom of God to arrive at the desired destination God has prepared for us.

The main challenges in which we need God's wisdom during transition are as follows: we will always face the challenge of something we do not know, we will always face the challenge of something that makes us very uncomfortable, and we will always face the challenge of something highly uncertain.

**First**, there is the challenge of SOMETHING UNKNOWN. In Israel's case it was the desert/wilderness. It was not familiar to them, and it required a walk of faith if they were to survive.

Every transition will require a new level of trust in God. You feed your faith on the Word of God. Your experience with God that has brought you this far will not take you through transition. Your experience must deepen, and your faith must get stronger to make it through unfamiliar territory.

**Second**, there is the challenge of SOMETHING UNCOMFORTABLE. The children of Israel were in an environment that was not hospitable. Every need had to be met by God.

When we move from our comfort zone we often find an environment that is hostile to any advancement. Sometimes this type of environment will drive us back to the area of comfort.

We are always saddened when we walk away from our dream. We might even think we are worse off than we were before transition started. We even start to murmur and complain about this journey. At this point we must remember that God's direction is always forward... NEVER RETREAT.

**Third**, there is the challenge of SOMETHING UNCERTAIN. The children of Israel were moving on to a new place where none of them had ever been before. Joshua 3:4 says:

> *Yet there shall be a space between you and it, about two thousand cubits by measure: come not near unto it, that ye may know the way by which ye must go: for ye have not passed this way heretofore.*

It was not left for Joshua to invent a method of crossing the flooded Jordan, for God gave him all the necessary instructions. The key word in this chapter is *ark*, used ten times. Of course, the ark symbolized the presence of God. The ark went before the people to lead them, and it was kept in the midst of the river until all the nation had passed over.

Christ always goes before His people and opens the way, but the people must sanctify themselves and be ready for God's leading. God was going to lead the Jews in a new way, and they had to be ready.

Above all, know that God is already where you are going. He is the alpha and omega, the first and the last, the beginning and the ending. Alpha and omega are the first and last letters of the Greek alphabet; they form a boundary for every Greek word. Jesus is "every word" you will need for transition.

# CHAPTER 17

DURING TRANSITION REMEMBER...

## YOU'RE JUST PASSING THROUGH

You will never rise above the current of information flowing into your life. If I can discover the quality of the information flow in your life, I can know the degree of dreams you will achieve. There must be a flow of information that you believe in order to pass through transition.

As you face the indicators of transition we just covered, it is imperative a person in transition remember key principles taught in God's Word. Let's look at some of these principles:

> *But now thus saith the LORD that created thee, O Jacob, and he that formed thee, O Israel, Fear not: for I have redeemed thee, I have called thee by thy*

> *name; thou art mine. When thou passest through the waters, I will be with thee; and through the rivers, they shall not overflow thee: when thou walkest through the fire, thou shalt not be burned; neither shall the flame kindle upon thee* (Isaiah 43:2).

These verses give Israel the assurance in eloquent detail that Christ gives to His church, that the gates of Hades will not prevail against it. Fire and water, peoples and distances, can take no toll; everyone will safely arrive whom God calls "Mine."

Exodus from Egypt was transition; the story of a people moving from one place/experience to another.

This text from Isaiah chapter 43 uses some key words and phrases. Notice:

• **Creation**: You are a "God product." That's what motivates God's interest in you. You are a result of God's planning and God's thinking. That should improve our self-esteem. God scheduled your birth. He planned on you being here, and He sowed gifts in you. Now, you must grow those gifts.

• **Redemption**: A price was involved to buy you back from satanic influence. We are restored.

God's a reaching God; He is an extrovert, not an introvert. He is a people person. God is not only a historian, He is prophecy. He looks at where we are going, not just where we have been. He does not only look at what we are, He looks at what we are to become.

• **Identification**: "Calls us by name." The antichrist system is a number system; the Jesus Christ system is a name system. I am a child of God, not a statistic. A statistic has no personality and no flexibility, but I do. God is not ashamed to be called our God. He is not embarrassed to be associated with us.

• **Possession**: "Thou art mine." God is sensitive about that subject. He identifies us as His property. Anything that touches us, touches Him. Don't speak evil of those of the household of faith. Anything that belongs to God, we should not touch... tithes, ministries, or persons; don't mess with God's stuff.

During transition, when God sees satan's attack coming at you, don't think for a minute He has not scheduled its failure. That's why He said, "No weapon that is formed against you shall prosper" (Isaiah 54:17).

• **Protection**: The God who set you in motion, will maintain your progress.

Isaiah 43:2 says, "When thou walkest through the fire." Let's break it down.

• **When**: Not "if." No adversity is surprising to God. No matter what others do to you, it does not surprise God. I don't care how many promises you know, you will taste "fire." You will walk through fire. That's part of transition—part of the process.

Your information flow is often distorted and based on your present feelings. When you are "down" everything is magnified.

• **Walkest**: Progression shows change in our life—even a constant change. We don't homestead in the fire. We are making progress. The fire is a place of purification. It is not a place of permanence; it is a place of passage.

One of satan's favorite tricks is to make you think you will stay in the fire forever. You can't see a favorable change. Stay connected with Jesus, and you will walk on through.

The second day of your trial, you are not the same person. The longer you are in a trial; God is at work with and in you. You are not stationary.

Transition is not a "pain tolerance test." God is processing an ingredient, in you, call greatness.

• **Through**: There is a scheduled day of completion. There is a "time period" in the fire—a season. 1 Corinthians 10:13 says that God makes a way of escape—from temptation and from the fire. Stay connected to God. Remember that Jesus completed the defeat of satan after three approaches.

Pain precedes pleasure. Adversity precedes advancement. Pain precedes promotion. Check out Daniel, Joseph, or Jesus. Pain is the packaging for pleasure. "For the joy that was set before Him endured the cross" (Hebrews 12:2).

Every experience to the fire cannot compare to the dimension of pleasure I have known when I came out.

If your world comes apart, stay connected to God; it will enlarge your pleasure. God is a God of progression. He didn't give us oak trees, He gave us acorns. Never quit. Don't be a "know it all." Stay close to Jesus. GOD WILL NEVER DISCONNECT!

### How to Transition Through the Fire Experience

There are a couple of significant disciplines to remember as you process through seasons of discomfort. Each discipline will require total focus in order to hasten the completion of one season and entrance into the next.

Discipline number **one**: Refuse to panic. God will compensate for any loss. Fear is a feeling of anticipated loss. God never guaranteed that loss would not happen; however, God said He would compensate. The Bible teaches there is a thirty, sixty, and hundred-fold blessing that can come into the life on one who sows. In transition, you are sowing part of your life, will, and emotions. Anticipate a harvest.

Discipline number **two**: Determine the reason for the fiery trial. It is not always the devil's fault; sometimes it's you. Resist any temptation to assign the responsibility of your loss to God. You are in control of your decisions. Your circumstances are created by your decision. When he was in trouble Daniel's decision was to pray.

Three Hebrew children decided not to bow. Decisions have consequences. Perhaps this trial is caused by a lack of knowledge. Prayer can put you back in the will of God. If a simple prayer can change a sinner, why can't it change your position? Any time satan gives you attention, God is getting a miracle close to your life. Daniel prayed for twenty-one days. God released the answer on the first day, but warfare was needed to get it through.

Warfare is necessary to navigate transitional seasons. I've never talked to anyone who outgrew warfare, or who obtained a maturity level where warfare did not exist. It is necessary to learn to fight. You will have to fight through fatigue, pressure, and many emotions that will scream doubts in your mind, but God remains faithful and focused on your life. His commitment is to get your through this season because the real battle is never over what you've done, it's always about where you are going and your next assignment. Hell fears your next assignment!

# CHAPTER 18

DURING TRANSITION REMEMBER...

## YOUR NEXT ASSIGNMENT IS COMING UP

A critical part of transition is when you have left your last assignment and are on the way to your next assignment. What makes this a critical moment is when the next assignment doesn't open quickly enough, and you find yourself between assignments. That's when you begin to hear the enemy's voice telling you how you've failed, your life is over, you've not heard the voice of God, and you'll never again become what you were before. He will also remind you that you were once busy about the Master's work, but now you sit idle with nothing of significance happening in your life.

In this critical moment of inactivity, when the next assignment seems unobtainable, it's easy to fall into depression.

Now, it's time to reveal your enemy's tactics. He is a deceiver and liar; he will attempt to wear you down and get you to quit. Please keep in mind that the opinion of others may not be accurate during this critical time of inactivity. Well-meaning friends may misunderstand your inactivity and side with the voices of the enemy, which are driving the depressing thoughts.

**This paragraph could be one of the most important to read for anyone in a transitional season.** It is imperative to understand this time of inactivity and isolation, along with feelings of loneliness. You need this time of stillness for God to flush the residue of previous assignments in order to bring a fresh anointing for the next assignment. Throughout the previous assignment some things attached to your life that are not needed, nor necessary, for the next assignment. Pain, hurt feelings, bitterness, fatigue, and a plethora of emotional baggage attach through any season of service to others. God chooses this time of inactivity to flush the residue of yesterday and use the clean vessel in which to pour a fresh anointing for the paradigm shift to bring the next assignment.

During this "in between" time, your enemy will distort information coming into your life and cause you to accept as truth, thoughts that are not true. He will also divert your attention from the destination of your journey to the mundane circumstances of this present time. Another weapon your enemy might use is the postponement or delay of the manifestation of the upcoming assignment.

During these attacks be sure to **stay focused on God's Word and His voice** within your recreated spirit. Contend for the truth of God's promise to come to pass. Dreams really do come true!

**Soak up information of intelligent people**. When you are drowning, the last thing you want to do is read a book on swimming. The discipline to gather this needed information will not be easy. The desire to hide in a cave is much more enticing, but don't; you need the information of wise people coming into your life.

This is the very best time to **release your own creativity**. God may give you a tremendous idea or connect you with important relationships at this critical time. Often, what you walk through will help define your destiny. As you overcome each battle, qualities are released within your life experience that will assist others along their journey. You are not going to be destroyed during transition. Within your own creativity are found keys to exit this present circumstance and facilitate the journey of destiny.

**Avoid a vocabulary of suffering**. You will attract buzzards. Stop talking "loser talk." For every person you attract, you will lose many that will help you. Nobody gave Job anything when he was down. When he got up, friends brought gifts. IF YOU CONSTANTLY TALK THE VOCABULARY

OF A VICTIM, YOU WILL DRAW A PREDATOR. It isn't necessary to advertise the trial. Job's three friends never visited until he lost everything. God will send people. Don't advertise; you will attract pain-lovers. Half the people don't care and the other half believe you deserve it. Find those who believe in you.

**Find somebody you can help, who is going through his or her own difficulty**. What you make happen for others, God will make happen for you. In 1 Kings 17 the Bible tells how a widow woman helped Elijah, and then God gave her miracle. Sow something into someone's life today. Seed sowing is a Bible principle; not just the law of sowing, but also the law of sowing and reaping.

**Know the signs or indicators of transition**, and adjust your thinking and believing to accommodate a successful season of transition. Transition is not a bad experience, it's a time of processing which releases the greatness God put in you before you were in your mother's womb.

# CHAPTER 19

DURING TRANSITION REMEMBER...

## PASSION IS THE FUEL TO GET YOU TO THE OTHER SIDE

*And a woman having an issue of blood twelve years, which had spent all her living upon physicians, neither could be healed of any, Came behind him, and touched the border of his garment: and immediately her issue of blood stanched. And Jesus said, Who touched me? When all denied, Peter and they that were with him said, Master, the multitude throng thee and press thee, and sayest thou, Who touched me? And Jesus said, Somebody hath touched me: for I perceive that virtue is gone out of me. And when the woman saw that she was not hid, she came trembling, and falling down before him, she declared unto him before all the people for what cause she had*

> *touched him, and how she was healed immediately. And he said unto her, Daughter, be of good comfort: thy faith hath made thee whole; go in peace* (Luke 8:43-48).

In this passage, we see a woman whose passion obtained what desire could never have on its own.

There is a difference between "desire" and "passion." ***Webster's New World Dictionary*** defines *desire* as: to wish or long for; crave; covet. That same dictionary defines *passion* as: extreme compelling emotion; intense emotional drive or excitement and enthusiasm. It goes on to record *passion* as a strong emotion that has overpowering or compelling effect. It also denotes fervor of burning intensity, restlessness, or flame-like emotion.

Transition is not a time to lose your passion. Passion is different than desire. Desire is when you want something. Passion is what you are unwilling to live without.

Jesus had no intention of healing this woman that day; she was not on his agenda. He was not even looking for her. Her passion determined what she could receive from the Lord. Therefore, we can say that passion has something to do with deciding the seasons of your life. How does one activate passion during a season when there is no incentive to believe that anything good can happen? You choose to remember the Word that God spoke to you during the time of refreshing.

Faith is your activator. There are some things you should remember about your faith. Your faith is an invisible substance; like wind, or electricity, you may not see it with your natural eye, but its presence and force are proven by its results in your life. You already possess the seed of faith within you; believing ability is within every person. You choose whether you use it for negative belief or positive belief.

When you use your faith, you please God. Do you appreciate it when others trust you? Imagine how God must feel when you trust Him. Your circumstances will change when you change the direction of your believing. You will, without doubt, experience what you consistently expect. Your biggest mountain will surrender to your smallest beginning of faith. It is important to actively pursue what you really believe God wants you to possess. Faith always draws the attention of God. Faith always stimulates incredible favor from God. Faith is the supernatural ingredient of every miracle. Faith comes when you hear something God says. Faith is like a muscle; the more you use it, the stronger it becomes.

With your passion activated, you can begin to move mountains that stand between you and the future God has promised. Passion can expedite transitional seasons. Transition seasons are important issues for the people of God. History is filled with accounts of God working through prophetic vessels to "make a way out" when there seems to be no possible way. Desire alone might not be enough to get you through a transition season successfully. You must release passion from your recreated spirit that will serve as your fuel/energy to get you to the other side.

### God Hears the Cry

The exit seems to be tied to a "travail and cry" which comes before a release. The travail and cry is more than a desire for an intended end; it is a passionate pursuit of that end. Exodus 2:23-25 says:

> *And it came to pass in process of time, that the king of Egypt died: and the children of Israel sighed by reason of the bondage, and they cried, and their cry came up unto God by reason of the bondage. And God heard their groaning, and God remembered his covenant with Abraham, with Isaac, and with Jacob. And God looked upon the children of Israel, and God had respect unto them.*

Pharaoh's death set the stage for Moses to return to Egypt, where his people were still being oppressed. When the Israelites cried out in their distress, God "remembered" His promise to Abraham and his descendants. *Remembered* does not mean that God had forgotten the Israelites. The Hebrew word is more closely translated to "concentrate on" or "act on." It was their passionate cry, not just a desire that brought the result they needed. This "cry" resulted in a transition for Israel, as well as Moses.

The struggle for the Israelites was that what they carried in their spirit was dramatically different from the life they were presently living. There was a contradiction between who they believed they were and where they found themselves. Their groaning was born out of the internal ambiguity that tormented them day and night. It was their season of transition. If the children of Israel had not cried out, God would not have sent them a deliverer! The prophetic voice of Moses was the result of God hearing the cry of the people, and remembering His covenant with their fathers.

The time had now come for the deliverance of Abraham's descendants from bondage and oppression in Egypt.

> *Now therefore, behold, the cry of the children of Israel is come unto me: and I have also seen the oppression wherewith the Egyptians oppress them. Come now therefore, and I will send thee unto Pharaoh, that thou mayest bring forth my people the children of Israel out of Egypt* (Exodus 3:9-10).

Moses' unique worship experience would lead to a forty-year work experience! The "cry" was a people instinctively asking for an "exodus event." They were passionate about a transition. The "cry" was their faith manifesting as a groan. They were passionate in releasing their faith at another level. The "cry" was the voice that could not merge, "who they were" with "where they found themselves." They were passionate to reach a literal place that matched what they felt in their heart.

The transition of Moses was born out of the "passionate groan of a people." Moses allowed something to become possible that was outside the realm of possibility. Your transition experience will often cause you to follow God into, what appears to be, a "dead end" only to discover that the "dead end" is actually a "doorway" to the next dimension. There are still many people who love God, but remain enslaved in areas of their lives. There must be a manifested, passionate, groundswell of groaning from deep within to produce a transition season.

Only two other times in the history of the world was there such chaos. In both instances, there was a prophetic voice which had to be protected, which rose up to speak to the people of God. They were both voices that provided instruction that guided a people safely through transition. Both Moses and Jesus were supernaturally protected in order that they might be raised up out of the presence of a death sentence on their generation to work an exodus in the appropriate season. Moses brought Israel out of Egypt, and Jesus opened a way for salvation.

Don't ever think, "It could never happen again!" As passionate groaning goes up, we will begin to hear breakthrough testimonies of openings which appear in the lives of many who were stopped at a dead end with NO WAY OUT! Your passionate groaning will produce your deliverance. Your NO WAY OUT will find a way. I am calling seasons of transition a bridge between assignments. It is a time of flushing away the residue of a previous assignment, and you receiving the anointing for the next assignment.

# CHAPTER 20

DURING TRANSITION REMEMBER...

## UNUSUAL PROVISION HAPPENS

> *And Elijah the Tishbite, who was of the inhabitants of Gilead, said unto Ahab, As the LORD God of Israel liveth, before whom I stand, there shall not be dew nor rain these years, but according to my word. And the word of the LORD came unto him, saying, Get thee hence, and turn thee eastward, and hide thyself by the brook Cherith, that is before Jordan* (1 Kings 17:1-3).

1 Kings 18:1 goes on to say. "And it came to pass after many days, that the word of the LORD came to Elijah in the third year, saying, Go, shew thyself unto Ahab; and I will send rain upon the earth."

Elijah experienced **three disciplines** during this three-year period. Transitional seasons usually provide opportunities to experience the same disciplines of Elijah. Each brought qualities out of Elijah that served as keys to the process and ultimately brought him to the moment of confrontation, which demonstrated the great miracle of God.

## Elijah's Brook

The beginning transitional lesson was at the brook and involved UNUSUAL PROVISION. Elijah found that as he was obedient to God, unusual provision would be part of the journey. In his obedience of hiding, God took care of Elijah. Earlier in this book in chapter eighteen, I mentioned the "down time" between seasons, or the occasion of "inactivity" that would appear. During this "in between" time, God provided unusual provision for His servant. Regardless of what part of transition you find yourself, God will always provide. Trust Him and know He will be faithful to His servants.

Remember the earlier lesson? "In Him we live, and move, and have our being." The brook is represented by the verb "LIVE." It also represents the first trimester of carrying your dream, the season of "limitation." The Lord permitted Elijah to drink of the brook, and He provided bread and meat daily, delivered to the prophet by ravens. The raven is the first bird named in the

Bible; it was an unclean bird, yet God used it to help His servant. It became a season of "unusual provision."

A day came when the brook dried. Did this mean Elijah had sinned, or that he was out of God's will? No! It simply meant that God had another place for him, and it was a reminder for Elijah to trust the Lord and not the brook. It's interesting to note that during a season of transition there is a conflict between God and your enemy. The enemy wants to stop your next assignment, and God wants to promote you.

Often the skirmish which takes place causes you to believe you are alone, and perhaps you have missed the will of God. It's at this time that you must be alert and look for "unusual provision."

This battle between God and Baal was felt most by Elijah. I'm sure he felt as though he was the "middle man." It reveals why we feel caught in a situation that requires miraculous provision to be sustained. Brooks were significant during transition times. Remember when spies were sent to view Canaan when Israel was in a time of transition? The Bible records their findings close to a brook.

> *And they came unto the brook of Eshcol, and cut down from thence a branch with one cluster of grapes, and they bare it between two upon a staff; and they*

> *brought of the pomegranates, and of the figs* (Numbers 13:23).

*Eshcol* means "cluster." The spies searched the land and even brought back some of the wonderful fruit, but they also brought back an evil report and discouraged the hearts of the people.

Be careful how you read the circumstances of transition. Ten spies read circumstances through their earthly senses, but two spies read the circumstances through faith. Sometimes transition can distort circumstances unless we remain in our faith walk. Except for Moses, Caleb, and Joshua, nobody in the nation believed that God would keep His promises! These three men saw this as a season of unusual provision. The ten unbelieving spies illustrate many believers. They have "spied out" their inheritance in Christ and have even tasted some of the fruits of His blessing; but their unbelief keeps them from entering in by faith.

The cluster of grapes was so large and so heavy that they hung it upon a bar, and they carried it between two of them. The place where they took it was called the valley of the cluster, that famous cluster which was to Israel both the earnest and the specimen of all the fruits of Canaan. Such are the present comforts which we have in communion with God—foretastes of the fullness of joy that we expect in the heavenly Canaan. All this happened close to the brook Esheol, the brook of "cluster." Israel ultimately received their unusual provision.

## David's Brook

Here is another significant transition season that involves a brook:

> *And he took his staff in his hand, and chose him five smooth stones out of the brook, and put them in a shepherd's bag which he had, even in a scrip; and his sling was in his hand: and he drew near to the Philistine* (1 Samuel 17:40).

Everyone's attention usually focuses on Goliath or David in this story. Some even try to describe the tension of the battle. I would rather focus on the brook that had hidden stones. Some have taught that Goliath had four brothers and David took five stones in order to defeat the brothers of Goliath. I would rather believe the five smooth stones taken from the brook represent a New Testament five-fold ministry. The ministry of the apostle, prophet, evangelist, pastor, and teacher were given by God to perfect the saints for the work of the ministry.

I believe those five smooth stones represent the type of ministry that will facilitate your journey of transition. The stones were smooth because they had been in the water a long time. The Bible says we (the church) are sanctified and cleansed by the washing of water by the word. In this story, three men, Saul, Goliath, and David are in transition. David, choosing five smooth stones, is the one who obtained an unusual provision.

### Jesus' Brook

Let's cover one final brook, as it has to do with transition. John 18:1 says, "When Jesus had spoken these words, he went forth with his disciples over the brook Cedron, where was a garden, into the which he entered, and his disciples." *Cedron* means turbid, cloudy, muddy, thick, dense, or dark from having the sediment stirred up. Certainly transition has produced such a time in everyone's life. In the life of Jesus, transition happened on His way to the cross. It was just before Gethsemane. Jesus was between the upper room of the last supper and Gethsemane. Transition is everywhere.

Jesus made it through transition to the glory. Look at Hebrews chapter 11 to find others who made it through transitional seasons. Each one mentioned received an uncommon provision during their transition. You can make it through. Embrace the season, but be on high alert. Let your spirit soar, be expectant, take another step, don't stop. Your next assignment is on the horizon. Remain strong and faithful. There is unusual provision at hand. Don't miss these strategic moments!

# CHAPTER 21

DURING TRANSITION REMEMBER...

## UNUSUAL PRESSURE HAPPENS

From 1 Kings 17:1-3, we note the three disciplines Elijah experienced during a transitional season of his life and ministry. The brook was the first, which represents unusual provision; now comes the barrel, which represents unusual pressure. This is another discipline he masters while in hiding or removed from public life.

Remember the earlier lesson? "In Him we live, and move, and have our being." The brook is represented by the verb "LIVE." Now, the barrel is represented by the verb "MOVE." It can also represent the second trimester of carrying your dream, which is the season of preparation.

God's Word always leads God's servant in the time of testing. But what strange commandments: 'Go to Gentile territory where a widow will feed you.' He was instructed to go to *Zarephath*, which means "refining;" God was certainly putting his servant through the furnace. Imagine Elijah's feelings when he discovered how poor the widow was and that she was about to prepare her last meal. It is a transition time for Elijah—as well as the widow—with unusual pressure on both parties, and God provided for her, her son, and her guest. Some days you are Elijah, other days you are the widow!

Unusual pressure will often reveal God's voice speaking to someone else about you. Zarephath was situated between Tyre and Sidon—the very center of the Baal cult. It was there that Elijah would demonstrate God's power to provide flour, oil, and rain, which were blessings customarily attributed to Baal. Also, this section emphasizes that God can protect the faithful, in this case, Elijah and the widow, even when they were outside the land of Israel. This would be a powerful lesson that God can bless his faithful people anywhere. God's Word works anywhere and in any adversity. During times of unusual pressure, be sure to remain on the foundation of what God has said to you in His Word.

One indication of the validity of our faith is its impact on individuals. Today, as in Elijah's day, the messenger of God must bring compassion and healing, as well as truth. Isaiah 48:10 says,

"Behold, I have refined thee, but not with silver; I have chosen thee in the furnace of affliction." The captivity was like being in a furnace to test them, not destroy them. If God would go back on His word about the return, His reputation would be defamed. The heat of the furnace would take out impurities and leave pure that which remains. It seems God affirms His choice of us when we are going through unusual pressure. Unusual pressure is part of transition.

## The High Place

Take a look at another point of transition in God's Word:

> *And after six days Jesus taketh Peter, James, and John his brother, and bringeth them up into an high mountain apart, And was transfigured before them: and his face did shine as the sun, and his raiment was white as the light. And, behold, there appeared unto them Moses and Elias talking with him* (Matthew 17:1-3).

Jesus took three of His disciples up into a high place. Transition does not only happen in low places; sometimes it happens in high places! If you are unwilling to go to the high places with God, you might miss some supernatural moments. Days of uncommon pressure require we go to high places in the Spirit in order to make it through the season.

On the mount we see Moses, who represented the Law; he had a part, but it was not complete. There was Elijah, who represented the Prophets; he had a part, but it was not complete. Then, there was Jesus, the Finisher; He takes the unfinished work from two who did their part only and cried, "IT IS FINISHED!" When each one has gone through transitional seasons and completed all within their ability, Jesus takes the unfinished part and brings it to completion. Moses and Elijah did the possible, but it took Jesus to do the impossible. The same principle works today. When you have done all you can (the possible), then God steps in to do the impossible.

## Life's Changes

Jesus was transfigured before them. The idea is a change of form. It really presents the essence of a thing as separate from an outward accident. There was a revealing of the true character of Jesus; His outer shell opened to reveal the true inner person. In Romans 12:2, Paul encourages transformation in the inner life. Unusual pressure produces changes in the inward man, as well as in the outward man. Unusual pressure also attracts a manifestation of the glory of God. Remember the following occurrences:

The glory seen in the transfigured Christ was the same glory cloud that shone in both the Tabernacle and the Temple. It was later withdrawn because of Israel's sin but then returned to confirm Christ's birth to the shepherds and to receive Christ at his ascension. Stephen would see God's glory (Acts 7:55), as would Paul (Acts 9:3) and John (Revelation 1:16).

The Transfiguration was, first of all, a picture of the coming kingdom. Jesus promised that some of the disciples would not see death until they had seen His kingdom. Another purpose was to strengthen Christ for His suffering. Moses and Elijah talked with Him about His coming "decease" or exodus at Jerusalem, and the voice of the Father came as another encouragement to the Son. It was also an encouragement to the disciples as they faced separation from the Lord as He experienced His suffering and death. Had they remembered this scene, they would not have failed Him or lost hope when He died.

Transitions produce many changes. The Bible is full of illustrations of transitional seasons and experiences which provide life lessons for us today. The following story illustrates the dramatic, and sometimes unusual, pressures that come quickly during transitions. Life gets "off schedule" when transition is taking place. Things happen that are not on the calendar. You sometimes have to deal with issues that are unpleasant surprises.

## New Heights

Here is a story about the pilot of a small airplane. While taking the plane up for a flight, the pilot heard a noise behind the instrument panel of the cockpit. He sent a radio message to the tower about the noise and received the following information: Sometimes, when the plane is parked and being serviced, as much as we try to keep it from happening, a rat or mouse can get inside the plane and usually heads for the wires behind the instrument panel. Sorry, but you have a rat on board and he could be chewing the wires behind the panel. The pilot's request was to land the plane immediately.

The response of the tower was unusual, "Don't land the plane, and instead take the plane as high as you can, as quickly as you can." The pilot didn't understand, he wanted to land the plane before the rat could chew through the wires and cause a crash. The tower instruction remained the same: "Take the plane as high as you can as quickly as you can."

The pilot reluctantly obeyed the instruction. He took the plane higher and higher. The plane began to shake violently as it maximized the limits of its ability. The pilot experienced new fears as the plane was forced into dimensions beyond its capacity. Suddenly the pilot refused to take the plane higher as it would be destroyed. The man in the tower had only one more question, "Do you hear the noise behind the instrument panel anymore?" The pilot's response was, "No, I don't hear the noise anymore." "Now, you can come back and land the plane," the man in the tower responded.

After the plane was on the ground, the technicians checked behind the instrument panel and, sure enough, they found a dead rat. The pilot questioned the men to find out why they wanted him to take the plane higher instead of bringing it back to land. The pilot was told the following: "Rats can't live at high altitudes, so we sent you higher to destroy the rat before bringing you back for the landing!"

The spiritual implication is clear. Sometimes, during transitional seasons, God will ask you to go to new heights. At the time it could seem improper and just simply crazy. God knows that rats can't live at high altitudes. Usually, when God takes you higher, His motive is to get rid of some rats in your life!

In 1 Kings 17, the barrel is only significant in that we see Elijah, during a time of transition, enduring unusual pressure. In your transition seasons, you will face unusual pressure. How you handle this season will largely determine your future.

In every instance, unusual pressure caused people to remember and lean on the Word of God. It's not complex; it's basic. Remain strong and focused, be ruthless with distractions, and see the salvation of the Lord.

# CHAPTER 22

DURING TRANSITION REMEMBER...

## UNUSUAL MIRACLES HAPPEN

Now, we come to the final discipline Elijah mastered during this transitional season. This is a time when unusual miracles happen. We can now identify the three stages of transition: limitation, preparation, and manifestation. In the final discipline before the next assignment, there is great discomfort. The dry brook was Elijah's test; the dead boy was the widow's test. Great testing usually follows great blessings.

During transition you will find many of your fellow travelers go through some of the same events, experience much of the same pressures, and have the same need for miracles as you.

"Give me the boy" is Elijah's answer, for he knew God could raise the dead boy to life again. This is the first recorded instance of resurrection in the Bible. Notice that he agonized for the boy and even stretched his own body upon his dead body. This is a great example for us today of raising dead dreams in our own lives, as well as in the lives of others. The miracle brought forth a testimony of faith from the woman.

Your faith will be tested as you continue to minister to others. You will often have a moment when your faith must be released at another level. Fear not, go ahead and reach for the miracle.

The final decision of the woman was emphatic and confident. We read in 1 Kings 17:24, "And the woman said to Elijah, Now by this I know that thou art a man of God, and that the word of the LORD in thy mouth is truth." Elijah himself clearly had no idea why this tragedy had struck. His prayer shows him bewildered and angry; then he prayed for the boy's restoration.

Even though we don't always understand the events of transition, we can have confidence that there is an uncommon miracle hidden somewhere in the pain. In the midst of every pain, there is a promise, a miracle, and a way out.

His reason for stretching himself on the boy is not clear; perhaps he was simply trying to share the warmth of his body with the boy to encourage his return to life. But the boy's restoration was God's doing in response to Elijah's prayer. Elijah was fed miraculously, and yet that did not secure him from dealing with sickness and death. There are moments of transition when you feel you've done everything right, yet bad things still happen. You still need an uncommon miracle.

Another time of "aloneness" experienced by Elijah as he must find God for himself, and on behalf of the boy. There is no crowd, or praise team, or preacher to encourage him. He must trust...alone!

*Zarephath* was the town to which God sent Elijah. It was in Jezebel's homeland! What a message this teaches. When Baalism entered Israel, the result was a devastating drought that crippled the land. But when Yahweh's prophet entered a foreign land, he brought hope to a starving widow and even restored her son to life!

One indication of the validity of our faith is its impact on others. Today, as in Elijah's day, the messenger of God must bring compassion and healing, as well as truth. How significant that the prophet did not bring a massive food supply. The small amount of oil and meal proved to be sufficient for her needs; God miraculously stretched supplies to meet daily needs. It is the same for us today. Jesus calls us to depend on Him for "daily bread." How good to know that we can depend on Him.

# CHAPTER 23

DURING TRANSITION REMEMBER...

## YOUR TIME WILL COME

In 1 Kings chapters seventeen and eighteen, we see Elijah obeying two commandments from the Lord: "Go hide yourself" and "Go show yourself." Just because you get an instruction from the Lord, never assume there's not another one coming later. In between these two commands, Elijah had to process a season of transition that reveals many qualities which are important to learn.

The "Go Hide Yourself" speaks of his private ministry. Aloneness does not necessarily mean loneliness. People of God in transitional seasons will experience "aloneness," but it doesn't have to progress to loneliness.

Having delivered his message to Ahab, the prophet Elijah retired from public ministry for three years, and during this time, the Lord graciously cared for him. The obedient servant can always depend on his Master's faithful care. Transition often provides a time of aloneness. This was to be an ultimate contest between God and Baal. Baal-worshipers believed that their god was the god of rain. The drought, brought on by the true God, showed that He, not Baal, controlled the weather. This was a remarkable demonstration of God's superiority and of the total inadequacy and falsehood of Baal worship.

The next step in Elijah's transition was for his public ministry—"go show yourself." After times of aloneness, pressure, frustration, and many other emotions, Elijah's great moment is at hand. Having been trained and tested in private, the prophet is now ready for his public ministry, so God commands him to face wicked King Ahab. We must admire Elijah's patience as he waited three years to preach one sermon.

### Your Pivotal Season

There is a Greek word for "time" that has always served to bless me when going through tough seasons. That word is *kairos*, which means, "a pivotal season." Notice it has nothing to do with calendar time or clock time. It has to do with a season that brings a pivot from one direction, and moves you in another direction. It's a GOD MOMENT! Elijah did not miss his "kairos" moment; his time had come.

Your "kairos" moment will bring you in touch with a variety of circumstances, and people. You must keep going forward as you are closer to your next assignment. Be relentless in this pursuit. How you navigate this part of transition will largely determine the speed at which you will exit one season and enter the next. Remain strong as these final challenges can break your focus and cause delays in future destiny. Let's take a quick rundown of people you might encounter during your pivotal season.

While experiencing a "pivotal" season you might meet some people with less passion than you. Obadiah is a picture of the compromising believer, and his life is in direct contrast to that of Elijah. Obadiah was serving Ahab and trying to serve Jehovah secretly. Passion is fuel to the future. Never lose a passionate desire to pursue God's assignment for life and destiny. Celebrate passionate pursuit and associate with like-minded souls on this journey of life.

You may also meet some people with different priorities. Elijah was "outside the camp;" Obadiah was inside the court. Elijah knew the will of God; Obadiah did not know what was going on. While Elijah was laboring to save the nation, Obadiah was out looking for grass to save the horses and mules. One must keep priorities in order to enjoy victory in adverse circumstances.

Misplaced priorities can sabotage a future quicker than you might imagine. Take a "priority evaluation" break once in a while to be sure life and purpose remain in godly order.

There are also some with a personal agenda. When Elijah confronted Obadiah, the frightened servant did not trust the prophet. Obadiah felt the need to brag about his secret service to impress Elijah with his devotion. Alas, we have too much of Obadiah these days and not enough Elijah! Personal agendas will incapacitate a dream quickly. It's important to remember: **never allow your personal agenda to carry you where your character cannot keep you**. Remain humble before the Lord. He will navigate you to the next assignment with expediency.

A pivotal season often brings confrontation. Sometimes confrontation cannot be avoided. Elijah finally met with Ahab and the prophets of Baal. This contest was not between Elijah and Ahab; it was between God and Baal. The nation was "limping and tottering between two ways," and it was time to make a decision. Elijah asked for an impossible solution. When the servant of God obeys and trusts the Word of God, he need not fear failure. By the time of the evening sacrifice, it was obvious to all that Baal was a false god and could not answer. Confrontation may not be with an individual; it could be with internal voices that continue to feed false information into your thinking. You have to silence those inner voices speaking against God's Word to have the peace of God rule your heart again. Never be reluctant to deal with false thinking.

Your pivotal season is usually linked to the harvest of someone else in need. Elijah was not out only to reform the people; he wanted to revive them as well. First, he repaired the altar, which the people had permitted to fall down. This is the first step toward blessing and restoration, repairing the personal altar of devotion, the family altar, the altar of sacrifice, and communion with God. By using twelve stones, Elijah reminded the people of their unity, because for many years the nation had been divided. Elijah had four barrels of water emptied on the wood and sacrifice three times, which would mean twelve barrels of water. The prophet prayed a simple prayer of faith, and the fire of God consumed the wood, the sacrifice, the water, and the altar. Elijah told the king to get back home, for rain was on the way.

What we do with God in private is far more important than what we do for God in public. Our hidden life prepares us for our public life. Unless we are willing to go through such disciplines as the dry brook, the depleted barrel, and the dead boy, we will never have the victories of Mt. Carmel. "They that wait upon the Lord shall renew their strength" (Isaiah 40:31).

Between "hide yourself" and "show yourself," you will encounter a BROOK (a time of unusual provision), a BARREL (a time of unusual pressure), and a BOY (a time of unusual miracles), all of which will provide successful navigation through a season of transition, which you are to complete before your next assignment. Your time will come!

# CHAPTER 24

DURING TRANSITION REMEMBER...

## FINISH THE JOURNEY STRONG

I am intensely aware that seasons determine outcomes and the outcome of this season can catapult you to an upgrade in life and a fresh, new assignment. Those dreams buried deep within your spirit, which have been covered by time and the debris of many adversities, are coming to a due season. Your tenacity and endurance have been tremendous weapons in this journey. Notice the maturing of strength that has manifested.

The process when this journey began was to fight harder in order to win; now you have learned to fight smarter in order to win. The many shifts of this time have brought fresh knowledge and wisdom to make you more effective in future warfare. Never believe you are only a survivor of transition, you are more than a conqueror in transition.

Continue this exciting journey of faith knowing that as this new season arrives, the old season of struggle will subside. Only as you are able to see the new will the old pass away. A new thing has a tendency to eliminate anything that is old. Transition has compelled you to go places internally that you would have never imagined.

When you choose to make disappointments become appointments, transition can generate incredible hope in the midst of hopelessness, confidence in the midst of despair, peace in the sadness of betrayal, and it will also provide strong endurance in the face of tribulation.

Always remember, your dream is larger than a season of transition. Your dream will live much longer than any single season of your life. Continue to listen to the voice of the dream rather than the voices of friends, families, and enemies. Much of who you are is heavenly. Your voice, talents, gifts, and skills are all heavenly created. Refuse to build your life around circumstances, situations, and problems, but build it around God's purpose.

Your new life waits. Be aggressive and push forward. God still believes in you. He remains confident that His plan for your life will be completed. Although the journey has been tough, the remnants and residue of transition will drop from your thinking as the renewed mind dominates the future. The scars of transition become testimonies of victory as well as encouragement to others. Embrace the new and value this journey as preparation, not punishment. Champions know the significance of preparation. It's the preparation that separates the champion from the "would be" champion. Preparation carries levels of discomfort and pain. Champions are tested in battle and sometimes have scars. You, my friend, are a champion of God.

Since you've started reading this book, I have partnered with you in *SURVIVING THE CHALLENGES OF TRANSITION*. Our journey together has encountered the ebb and flow of seasonal changes. It is my sincere prayer that our partnership will not end when this final page is completed. This writing has been wrapped in prayer from the inception. Should the information found in *SURVIVING THE CHALLENGES OF TRANSITION* be of help in your journey, please take a moment and use the contact information below to share your testimony, or prayer needs. No one is an island to himself or herself. We need each other. Perhaps God has connected us for such a time as this!

Contact Information:
Bishop Gerald Doggett
www.geralddoggett.com

# DR. GERALD DOGGETT

DR. GERALD DOGGETT is a man with a vision...a vision to minister the Word of God to the nations by planting a church in every country and by deploying spiritual sons and daughters around the world. Gerald has served in various capacities of ministry, including pastor, teacher, apostle, and spiritual-overseer. He is the founder and president of Covenant Connection International through which he ministers to church leaders around the world. He and his wife Doris have been in ministry for over 40 years and currently reside in Orlando, Florida.

# COVENANT CONNECTION INTERNATIONAL & GERALD DOGGETT MINISTRIES

We are dedicated to the care and encouragement of ministers and their families. It is not a denomination or a typical ministerial fellowship. It is Apostolic in nature, based on covenant relationship and designed to enhance your ministry and assist you in reaching your full potential in the Kingdom of God.

**Our Mission**
To equip ministers and churches to reach their full potential in the Kingdom of God.

**Our Vision**
To deploy spiritual sons and daughters around the world and to plant churches in every nation.

**Our Strategy**

- Provide Apostolic covering for ministers, ministries and churches.
- Network ordained ministers together in covenant relationships for the purpose of fellowship, mentoring, accountability, and synergistic strength.
- Network churches of similar doctrine, worship expression, and vision for the purpose of promoting church development, growth, and multiplication.
- Mobilize ministers, churches, businesspersons, and the Body of Christ for the purpose of evangelism, church planting, and world missions.
- Synergize relationships and resources for the purpose of advancing individual churches and ministries.

**Parsons Publishing House**

*Your Voice Your World*™

## SURVIVING THE CHALLENGES OF TRANSITION

**by Dr. Gerald Doggett**

Dr. Doggett exhorts the reader to not let their past dictate their future. He provides exciting nuggets which include: It's OK to Remain A Chair!, Your Dream Will Attract Favor & Warfare, God Restores Everything That Has Been Lost!, Sometimes You Need to Have A Party! $12.95.

## PORTRAIT OF A PASTOR'S HEART

**A Manual on Caring for the Sheep**

**by Bishop Gerald Doggett**

This book is a must for pastors, elders, students & laymen who want to learn how to care for the flock of God. Bishop Gerald Doggett paints a rare and intimate portrait covering TOPICS such as: Spirit of a Finisher, The Necessity of the Divine Call and A Beautiful Portrait of Preparation. $12.95.

## WHY DO I DO THE THINGS I DO?

**Understanding Personalities**

**by Darrell Parsons**

In this insightful book, Darrell Parsons identifies the four primary types of personalities and how they interact together. As you grow in understanding, you will gain the tools you need for developing successful relationships in all areas of your life. $10.95.

## SILENCING THE ENEMY WITH PRAISE

**by Pastor Robert Gay**

In this book, you will learn what God's Word says about the power of praise to: destroy the strongholds of Satan; bring healing, deliverance, and restoration; release the prophetic word; win the victory in spiritual warfare; and drive out demonic principalities. $11.95.

## 70 REASONS FOR SPEAKING IN TONGUES

**by Bishop Bill Hamon**

Over 600 million Christians have received the Holy Spirit gift of tongues, and 95% of Spirit-baptized Christians only utilize 10% of the benefits of speaking in tongues. Learn how to use your spirit language to activate more faith and increase God's love and power within your life and ministry (216 pages). $14.95.

## 30 DAYS TO A BETTER PRAYER LIFE

**by Pastor Nora King**

Nora King offers fresh revelation and practical teaching to help you experience the release of God's power. You will learn daily how to improve your prayer life and enter God's presence through these simple principles. You don't have to struggle in prayer any longer! $11.95.

## RELEASE YOUR WORDS - IMPACT YOUR WORLD

**by Darrell Parsons**

Your words can make a difference! God has placed treasures inside you; learn to release them to influence your world. In this book, Darrell Parsons challenges you to use your voice to impact the world around you today. $9.95.

## THE EFFECTIVE PRAISE & WORSHIP LEADER
**by Dr. Ron Kenoly**

What is a good worship leader? What does a pastor want in a worship leader? Use this book as a measuring stick for the anointed person you want to become. From his vast experience, Ron Kenoly shares insight into the office of the worship leader. $10.95.

## The PRIORITY OF PRAISE & WORSHIP
**by Dr. Ron Kenoly**

Through this book, you will receive proven answers to common and uncommon issues from one of the nation's leading worship authorities. Each chapter is designed to take you to a higher level of excellence in your worship experience. $12.95.

## LIFTING HIM UP
**by Ron Kenoly & Pastor Dick Bernal**

Worship leader Ron Kenoly teams up with pastor, Dick Bernal, in this practical guide to praise and worship. You'll learn Bible how to enter into the Lord's presence, plus gain insight into the scriptural role of praise and worship in your life and church. $12.95.

## REVELATION: BEHIND THE VEIL
**by Rev. Laurin E. Young**

The book of Revelation has intrigued people through the years. Rev. Laurin Young shares his years of study in this chapter by chapter commentary on the Apocalypse. The rich spiritual truths serve as a "layman's commentary" and a good reference tool for teachers. $14.95.

**www.ParsonsPublishingHouse.com**

## CAPTURING THE HEART OF GOD
**Pleasing the Father in Everyday Life**
**by Diane Parsons**

God created man for His good pleasure. Make it your goal today to do those things which please God. This book contains practical tips on how capturing the heart of God and becoming His delight every day. $10.95.

## WITH EVERY BEAT OF MY HEART - A Weekly Devotional
**by Jeff North**

***Every Beat of My Heart*** takes the reader to a place where inspirational stories and poems stay upon their hearts and lips throughout the day. This book offers a practical message with a godly foundation to encourage, motivate and bring comfort (224 pages). $14.95.

## MEMOIR TO MY BOSOM BUDDY
**Journal of My Walk With Breast Cancer**
**by Janet Bergdoll**

Like thousands of other women, Janet was diagnosed with breast cancer. As a registered nurse, she underwent treatment by the book, and she journalled through her diagnosis, treatment, and recovery. The result is an inspirational book about her walk with breast cancer. $12.95.

## MOUNTAIN VIEW -A Photo Collection
**by Doris Beets**

Contained in these pages is a pictorial discovery of a community where splendor is exemplified. Doris Beets attempts to give you a glimpse of the world that captured her heart over 75 years ago. $29.95.